WITHDRAWN
UTSA Libraries

D0154172

The Quest
for Nuclear Stability

THE QUEST
FOR NUCLEAR STABILITY

John F. Kennedy
and the Soviet Union

Bernard J. Firestone

Contributions in Political Science, Number 73

Greenwood Press
Westport, Connecticut • London, England

Library of Congress Cataloging in Publication Data

Firestone, Bernard J.
  The quest for nuclear stability.

  (Contributions in political science, ISSN 0147-1066 ;
no. 73)
  Bibliography: p.
  Includes index.
  1. Arms control. 2. United States—Foreign relations
—Soviet Union. 3. Soviet Union—Foreign relations—
United States. I. Title. II. Series.
JX1974.F468   327.73'0092'4   81-13257
ISBN 0-313-23214-8 (lib. bdg.)   AACR2

Copyright © 1982 by Bernard J. Firestone

All rights reserved. No portion of this book may be
reproduced, by any process or technique, without the
express written consent of the publisher.

Library of Congress Catalog Card Number: 81-13257
ISBN: 0-313-23214-8
ISSN: 0147-1066

First published in 1982

Greenwood Press
A division of Congressional Information Service, Inc.
88 Post Road West, Westport, Connecticut 06881

Printed in the United States of America

10 9 8 7 6 5 4 3 2 1

Copyright Acknowledgments

Grateful acknowledgment is given for permission to quote from the
following:

Bundy, McGeorge. "The Presidency and the Peace." *Foreign Affairs* 42
(April 1964): 353-65. Reprinted by permission from *Foreign Affairs*, April
1964. Copyright 1964 by Council on Foreign Relations, Inc.

Destler, I. M. "Comment: Multiple Advocacy: Some 'Limits and Costs'."
The American Political Science Review 66 (September 1972): 786-90.
Reprinted by permission from *The American Political Science Review*,
September 1972. Copyright 1972 by the American Political Science
Association.

LIBRARY
The University of Texas
At San Antonio

To Howard H. Lentner

CONTENTS

PREFACE

This study attempts to understand the role of presidents in the formulation of American Cold War diplomacy and concentrates on the last year of John F. Kennedy's presidency. Historians disagree in assessing the achievements that marked the final year of this president's life. To Kennedy's critics, notably on the left, the Test Ban Treaty, the Hotline Agreement, and the Soviet grain deal were little more than liberal window-dressing for a conventional Cold War strategy that otherwise stimulated the arms race and escalated America's tragic involvement in Viet Nam. To admirers of the president, 1963 represented a year of change both in the Cold War and in Kennedy's conduct of American foreign policy, and they lament the president's death for arresting a trend toward global order that might otherwise have been realized in a second term.

Without supporting either of these two assessments, this study chooses to view the Kennedy détente as both an extension of his predecessors' Cold War legacy and as a transition to a more systematic treatment of the inherent ambivalences in U.S.-Soviet relations. Kennedy essentially embraced and even elaborated upon the military doctrine of containment, which had originated under Truman and Eisenhower before him. But like his predecessors, Kennedy sought to avert the catastrophe of nuclear war. What was distinctive about his presidency was Kennedy's effort to combine the objectives of anticommunism and nuclear war avoidance into a single military and political strategy—in the form of arms control. His successors—and it remains to be seen how Ronald Reagan will approach this issue—have since accepted, to one degree or another, the fundamental validity of Kennedy's conception of the national interest.

This book is divided into three parts. Chapter 1 examines the role of presidents as chief architects of American Cold War diplomacy. Chapters 2 through 6 look at Kennedy's foreign policy toward the Soviet Union and its climax, the détente of 1963. The epilogue links Kennedy's foreign policy to those of his successors. Source material includes a wide array of readily available secondary literature along with personal memoirs and voluminous records of congressional hearings. Most valuable was the contribution of the John F. Kennedy Library in Boston, Massachusetts, and its very capable and cooperative staff. The library provides a rich lode of original sources including interviews with governmental and nongovernmental personages and especially useful archival material. Some of the archival material was made available to me in August 1978 under the terms of the Freedom of Information Act. Unfortunately, other potentially relevant material was withheld on the basis of national security considerations. Special thanks to W. Averell Harriman, U. Alexis Johnson, and Benjamin H. Read for allowing me to cite from their oral history interviews.

I would like to take this opportunity to thank Professor Howard H. Lentner of the Graduate Center of the City University of New York for his invaluable assistance. I can never express adequately my deep debt of gratitude to him for his incalculable support. I would also like to extend my thanks to Professors Abraham Bargman and Arthur M. Schlesinger, Jr. Thanks also to the Political Science Department at Hofstra University for their strong encouragement, and to Marilyn Shepherd, Liz Shepherd, and Sheila Kurtzer, who typed various versions of this manuscript.

Finally, I would like to thank those members of my family who brought me to this point in my life—my father and mother, my brother Nate, my aunts Cillie and Judith, and my wife Dedi.

The Quest
for Nuclear Stability

1.
PRESIDENTS AND
THE NATIONAL INTEREST

Anticommunism, the driving force behind American foreign policy since the end of World War II, has survived extraordinary global and domestic changes to remain the predominant feature of the American national interest. The resilience of this theme is all the more striking when one considers the strides that have been made in amelioration of the tensions between the United States and the world's foremost Communist nation, the Soviet Union. While the late 1940s and early 1950s were characterized almost exclusively by confrontation, the late 1950s gave rise to episodic Cold War thaws that punctuated the continuing superpower rivalry with brief periods of détente. These early periods of détente set the stage for substantive negotiations in areas where the nuclear giants evolved complementary interests. In the 1960s, major arms control and trade agreements were signed, and in the 1970s, détente became, if only temporarily, part of the official lexicon of American foreign policy. Even as relations between the superpowers soured in the late 1970s, the two sides continued to treat arms control as a major priority and managed to conclude a treaty placing mutual limits on strategic weapons. The apparent demise of this treaty suggests the existence of serious domestic reservations about the terms of détente but does not—the rhetoric of the Reagan administration notwithstanding—indicate a permanent repudiation of the process of limited accommodation, which has been a persistent feature of American Cold War diplomacy.

Periodic relaxations of tensions and the discovery of ongoing mutual interests have not, however, attenuated the fundamental rivalry between the two great powers. American foreign policy, in particular, has been characterized by a strikingly ambivalent posture that fundamentally reflects the contradictory tendencies of a bipolar nuclear age. As a consequence, policies that have been directed toward easing superpower tensions have more often than not been juxtaposed with policies that seem to maintain or even reinforce existing strains. The Kennedy détente of 1963, for example, was preceded by an enormous expansion in the nation's strategic and conventional arsenal. The Nixon détente was accompanied by great technological growth in nuclear weapons and occurred simultaneously with the relentless effort to achieve a favorable settlement in Indochina through military means. The Second Strategic Arms Limitation Treaty (SALT II) was negotiated even as the Carter administration was deciding to develop and deploy the controversial MX missile system. This simultaneous alternation between accommodative and hard-line gestures has been and continues to be one of the most ill-defined and little understood features of American foreign policy. Today especially, as the nation's international fortunes are said to have undergone noticeable decline, these contradictions have become the subject of sharp criticism, contributing to fissional tendencies within the Western alliance, the apparent disintegration of détente, and the erosion of the foreign policy consensus at home. To its Western European allies, the American posture is one of dangerous irresolution. To its Soviet interlocutors, shifts in the American stance from accommodation to bellicosity undermine Washington's reliability as a negotiating partner. At home, American policy generates similar anxieties as ambivalence is mistaken for lack of purpose. In sum, few are satisfied with the contradictions in the American approach to the Soviet Union, which nevertheless have been a fixture of American foreign policy throughout the Cold War. They have endured changes in the Western alliance and in the strategic balance, oscillations in the public mood, and turnovers in the partisan identification of presidents and in the composition of the national security elite.

Despite the impression of inconsistency that critics of American foreign policy often ascribe to the American posture in the world, there are, in fact, compelling reasons why foreign policy ambivalences—particularly in regard to Soviet-American relations—are more calculated than accidental. The relationship between the United States and the Soviet Union is inherently ambiguous. Both nations are locked into an irrepressible antagonism by virtue of their competing ideologies, conflicting power interests, and the deadly threat that they pose to one another. At the same time, neither side can afford to pursue that antagonism to the point of direct military confrontation. Instead, the superpowers are compelled to act out their rivalry while seeking to avoid the holocaust of nuclear war. No American leader—no matter his aversion to war—can escape the military and political responsibilities associated with the Soviet challenge to the national security. At the same time, no president—no matter how intense his anticommunism—can for long ignore the need to seek a level of big power accommodation that will forestall the equally destructive threat of nuclear catastrophe. Hence, the alternation between confrontation and accommodation that recurs in the American posture toward the Soviet Union can be seen as a deliberate, even rational response to the conflicting exigencies of a fundamentally bipolar nuclear world.

The vast mainstream of American public opinion, both elite and mass, recognizes the importance of both goals—anticommunism and avoidance of nuclear war—to the nation's survival. At the same time, the consensus about goals is sufficiently broad to permit ongoing controversy regarding more limited objectives and strategies. For this reason, ambivalence is accentuated in the conduct of foreign policy. The effect of political considerations is to make the direction and character of policy murkier. But often what appears to be an inconsistency results from a deliberate presidential effort to maintain the appearance of "balance" by satisfying the disparate elements in his foreign policy constituency.

The ambivalence in American foreign policy can also be traced to the variety of bureaucratic interests and orientations that are involved in the process of policy formulation and implementation. The issue of Soviet-American relations is exceedingly complex, touching to one degree or another on almost all aspects of America's global interests. It is impossible to expect that each foreign policy problem should mobilize the same constellation of bureaucratic groups or arouse the same level of presidential, partisan, or public attention. Consequently, two results are readily distinguishable. First, in those areas of Soviet-American relations where there is significantly widespread organizational participation, there will inevitably be a need for compromise involving the reconciliation of opposing bureaucratic interests. Second, across a wide range of issues, policies will vary depending on the identities of those bureaucratic actors—including presidents—who are most heavily involved from one issue to the other in the process of policy formulation.

The effect of these three factors—the international system, the domestic setting, and bureaucratic politics—is to produce a high level of constancy in the American approach to the Soviet Union. The national interest, as a function of the international system, persists in mandating the pursuit of two primary goals: anticommunism and avoidance of nuclear war. The domestic political system, united in only the broadest sense around this dyadic conception of the national interest, continues to constrain policy that is allegedly too purposeful toward one side or the other. The bureaucratic apparatus pulls and tugs in numerous directions, so that policy is rarely uniform across a spectrum of issues. In sum, the centrifugal tendencies of a bipolar nuclear age and a loosely centered domestic political system combine to make ambivalence an ongoing characteristic of American Cold War diplomacy.

The Cold War has posed an unprecedented challenge to the formulation of a coherent national strategy. For the first time in its history the United States has been drawn into a protracted global and ideological struggle that has no forseeable resolution. Complicating the approach to this conflict has been the relative ineffectiveness of the traditional means of power, specifically warfare. In both world wars of the twentieth century the United States was able, once awakened to the threat from abroad, to compel its adversaries into submission. The Cold War, however, offers no such quick fixes. With their ultimate military tools virtually neutralized, American policymakers have been called upon to fight a deadly struggle on "ambiguous terrain."[1] They have been compelled to combat not only a relentless ideological adversary but also to prevent the outbreak of war in an age when technology has rendered the traditional means of power less utilitarian if not totally ineffectual. According to Paul Seabury, the nuclear age has turned von Clausewitz's famous aphorism around. Politics has now become the continuation of warfare by other means.[2]

The strains of this technologically and politically revolutionary age have been especially burdensome on presidents. Presidents have always borne a special obligation as commanders in chief. William McKinley, responding to the warmongering of his assistant secretary of the navy, Theodore Roosevelt, was said to have remarked, "I suspect that Roosevelt is right . . . and the only difference between him and me is that mine is the greater responsibility."[3] But the nuclear age has introduced

a new and awesome twist to the president's role as chief of the
armed forces. Traditionally, warfare, once initiated, shifted
from the province of the politician to that of the professional
military man. Presidents concerned themselves with shoring up
alliances and mapping out plans for a postwar world. The president was the chief diplomat, the military men his war makers.
In the nuclear age, however, presidents have become the ultimate instruments of destruction. They make the daily decisions
that adjudicate between instant war and a fragile peace. They
control the deadly forces of destruction that can be unleashed
with one command. Finally, they must secure the boundary
between conventional conflict and nuclear disaster. In a world
where the threshold between limited war and all-out destruction is so tenuous, the president, as guardian of that boundary,
is compelled to be extraordinarily sensitive to the cataclysmic
consequences of war. It is no wonder, then, that all American
presidents since Eisenhower have made the pursuit of peace
among their highest national priorities.

If presidents have been especially sensitive to the dangers
of nuclear war, they have also recognized that the security of
the state is inextricably linked to the possession of nuclear
weapons. No president has yet suggested—nor is one likely to
suggest in the future—that America unilaterally disarm as it
did in the period between the world wars. The almost certain
possibility that a first-strike nuclear attack by the enemy would,
in a matter of minutes, extinguish the nation's capacity for re-
groupment and retaliation makes a second-strike capability the
the only plausible assurance against destruction or surrender.
Thus, the avoidance of nuclear war has come to depend on the
maintenance of an equilibrium of military power between the
nuclear giants.

Deterrence alone has been seen, however, as too fragile a
mechanism upon which to base the nation's security. Unre-
mediated by arms control, the balance of terror is subject to
destabilizing shocks including the ever-present dangers of
preemptive or accidental war. To be sure, the United States
was slow to recognize the complementary interests of the Cold
War adversaries in this regard. Not until the Kennedy administration did an arms control theory really evolve to guide relations
between the superpowers. Since then, however, successive presidents, with the possible exception of Ronald Reagan, have defined the security of the state as requiring a situation of nuclear
deterrence stabilized by arms control.

Both nuclear deterrence and arms control flow from a perspective that views world politics in terms of power. According to this line of thought, potential aggressors, such as the Soviet Union, can be expected to exercise restraint in the face of equal or superior power. Moreover, ideological adversaries—insofar as they are balanced militarily—can negotiate and conclude agreements that touch on complementary interests. No less a cold warrior than Richard Nixon represented this approach when he wrote:

> Never once in my career have I doubted that the Communists mean it when they say their goal is to bring the world under Communist control. But unlike some anti-communists . . . I have believed that we can and must communicate and, when possible, negotiate with Communist nations. . . . We must always remember that they will never act out of altruism, but only out of self-interest. In fact, in January 1969 I felt that the relationship between the United States and the Soviet Union would probably be the single most important factor in determining whether the world would live at peace during my administration.[4]

This perspective is, however, inconsistent with the extreme ideological portrait of the Soviet Union that developed during the early days of the Cold War. According to the latter view, there can never be a complementarity of interests between the superpowers. Instead, the Soviets favor arms control only to gain a decided advantage in their struggle with the United States. The United States, on the other hand, cannot accept coexistence with an adversary whose political system is so morally repugnant and whose foreign policy violates all standards of justice that Americans subscribe to. This view, which was popular in the early days of the Cold War and is once again achieving some prominence, places a heavy burden on presidents who might seek to stabilize a situation of mutual nuclear deterrence through negotiation, or who might practice restraint in the use of American power.

Because presidents cannot escape the fundamentally ambivalent nature of the national interest, their role is to educate the public to the realities of the nuclear age even as they continue to pursue the Cold War in ideological terms. Presidents who favor arms control must convince the public that there are means other than nuclear war and an unrestrained arms race to resist communism. Presidents who favor unlimited defense spending and reject the logic of arms control must justify their restraint in specific situations where the range of options available to them is so limited. The management of these apparently contradictory strains in the national interest is a distinctly presidential enterprise. As Franz Schurmann noted in his thoughtful book *The Logic of World Order*, in the realm of nuclear politics—with its connotation of persistent crisis—the nation looks to the president for its sense well-being.[5] Because national security is a symmetrical issue that supposedly affects all people equally, a president, who transcends parochial interests, is in the best position to articulate consensual goals and allay national anxieties. In an age when security depends on the prevention of war as much as it does on the avoidance of surrender, the president must ultimately strike an ambivalent pose. He must convince the nation that while he is seeking sanctuary from nuclear war, he is not jeopardizing its security by encouraging Communist encroachments. To do so is no small task. Critics from the right and the left, governmental and nongovernmental, will inevitably accuse him of overvaluing one priority at the expense of the other. A president who deliberately chooses to disregard either of these two groups will ultimately find his political resources strained. A president who attempts to placate them by shifting abruptly from one side to the other will satisfy no one. A president, by dint of his institutional role, has no choice but to pursue a balanced strategy. He must mobilize the political system toward the acceptance of ambivalences as legitimate expressions of the national interest. To do so, while minimizing the appearance of inconsistency, is the true test of presidential leadership in the Cold War.

THE INTERNATIONAL SYSTEM AND THE COLD WAR

American foreign policy has undergone numerous alternations in the years following the close of World War II as presidents have grappled with the ever-present Soviet challenge in the face of dynamic global and strategic conditions. Included among these changes have been doctrines as varied as "massive retaliation" and "flexible response," "détente" and "brinkmanship," "cities avoidance" and "mutual assured destruction." Each of these policies has been subjected to intense scrutiny and debate, and each has at one time or another receded under the weight of public and elite attack. Despite the appearance of change, however, the basic thrust of these policies has been directed toward the achievement of a fairly consistent set of goals. Strategic and policy shifts have taken place within the context of a fundamental continuity in American foreign policy—a continuity that derives from the persistence of a systemically determined national interest.

A classic debate in the study of international politics involves the question often called the "level of analysis" problem.[6] Do statesmen act according to internal or external referents? In other words, what is the source of the so-called "national interest"? Political scientist Wolfram Hanreider offered a useful and interesting approach to this question when he identified three classes of actor objectives in international politics—internal, external, and systemic.[7] Internal objectives result from a combination of political, socioeconomic, and cultural values that are domestic in character. They can be unique to the nation or similar to values shared by other nations. Their definition does not require reference to other specifically identified actors or types of actors. External objectives can be formulated only in relation to other states. Goals such as ideological self-extension or supranationalism require significant reference to the external environment. Systemic objectives, which as opposed to external goals are nonnormative in character, result from the actor's subjective definition of the international arena, its constraints and opportunities. This assessment produces goals that are said to be systemically referred. The national interest, therefore, can be seen as a combination of internal, external, and systemic objectives. While the internal or external values may remain constant—or given unusual circumstances even change—the national interest as an aggregate must necessarily be responsive to transformations in the international environment.

Political scientist Arnold Wolfers defined one very important aspect of the national interest as involving "self-preservation," which he defined as "all demands pointing toward the maintenance, protection or defense of the existing distribution of values, usually called the status quo."[8] Hanreider expressed reservations about this definition because it did not sufficiently delineate among internal, external, and systemic values, and Wolfers acknowledged that the "national self . . . can undergo a wide variety of interpretations" and include a broad range of so-called vital interests.[9] Nevertheless, Wolfers argued that there are certain values—such as national survival, independence, and territorial integrity—that are so fundamental to the nation's existence that statesmen are almost unconsciously driven to protect them.[10]

National values are shaped by a variety of historical, social, and cultural determinants that go toward creating what might be referred to as a distinctive "way of life." When a statesman enters office, apart from a revolution, the expectation that he will sustain the prevailing norms is more compelling than any personal preference he might have. This expectation produces certain foreign policy imperatives over which the statesman has little control. The need, for example, to maintain a strong defense, either alone or through alliance, is mandated by the goal of self-preservation, no matter who the statesman is. The need to have power on the international stage and the need to avert national suicide through catastrophic war are similar requirements—although the latter has become even more important in the nuclear age. In other words, to borrow Seyom Brown's terminology, there is an "irreducible" national interest that defines the basic requirements of foreign policy and transcends changes in the personnel who might govern.[11] These requirements can undergo change with transformations in the international system, and they are broad enough to allow significant differences in interpretation, but at any given time they are both identifiable and compelling.[12]

The close of World War II saw an almost immediate breakdown in the wartime alliance between the major Western powers and the Soviet Union. It also produced a virtual bipolar relationship between the Soviet Union and the United States and a decline in the ability of traditional European powers to shoulder the load in the struggle against communism. While many revisionist scholars argue that American policymakers deliberately chose a policy of confrontation from among a range of options available to them, in fact a fairly broad consensus developed at the time around the proposition that the Soviet Union "threatened vital American security interests, mainly in Europe, through a combination of political and military subversion, backed up by military blackmail, during conditions of economic prostration."[13] It took some time and debate before policymakers could identify the exact nature of the threat and then settle on an appropriate response. Nevertheless, by the end of the Korean War, the military character of the Soviet challenge had become a national article of faith. Since then, constraint of Soviet power, involving the maintenance of an enormous and sophisticated defense apparatus, has remained the nation's chief foreign policy imperative.

According to Hanreider, systemic referents are most heavily influenced by perceptions and therefore one might imply, most subject to internal debate. The values that go toward producing internal and even external objectives are usually so ingrained in a society that they are invariably accepted as inevitable. In the case of the postwar situation facing the United States, values such as democracy at home and self-determination and free trade abroad were subscribed to almost uniformly. In formulating a new concept of the national interest, however, policymakers had to relate these relatively immutable goals to the changing circumstances of the postwar world. Here, varying perceptions operated to produce an initial vacillation in American foreign policy. Daniel Yergin in his *Shattered Peace: The Origins of the Cold War and the National Security State* distinguished between the "Riga" and "Yalta" axioms in the foreign policy establishment.[14] Exponents of the former viewed the Soviets as relentlessly expansionistic, determined to crush the sovereignties of small states, and ultimately to destroy democracy. The "Riga" advocates believed that there could be no accommodation with so implacable an enemy as Soviet Russia. Proponents of the "Yalta" axiom, while not entirely sanguine about Soviet behavior, reasoned that wartime accommodation could be extended into the postwar world. According to their point of view, the Soviets were less interested in violating self-determination than in establishing a security belt against renewed attack from the West. To extreme "Yalta" types like Henry Wallace, the threat to democracy at home came less from the Soviet Union than it did from a supercharged warfare atmosphere that a policy of confrontation would and inevitably did produce. Throughout Truman's first year as president, American foreign policy reflected this perceptual division by wavering between direct challenges to Soviet hegemony in Eastern Europe and methods by which the Soviets could be integrated into the new political order, particularly with regard to atomic energy.

Eventually a confluence of factors conspired to make the "Riga" axiom the principal engine of American Cold War policy. The lobbying efforts of bitterly anti-Soviet Eastern European ethnic groups and the hard-line drumbeats of the Republican party made it politically unfeasible for the Democratic president to pursue a policy of accommodation. Moreover, Soviet intractability on key postwar questions along with Stalin's in-

creasing rhetorical truculence made conflict inevitable. Soviet
behavior following World War II collided dramatically with
basic principles of American foreign policy and revived the
ideological animus between the great powers that had subsided
during the war. Soviet actions seemed to confirm the "Riga"
view of Soviet behavior—a view that gained ultimate confirmation in Ambassador George Kennan's celebrated "long cable"
to Washington. Perhaps most importantly, according to historian
John Gaddis, the American commitment to self-determination,
which Roosevelt had championed during the war, was deeply
offended by the Soviet refusal to allow free elections on its
borders.[15] This aspect of Soviet behavior, more than anything
else, generated profound public and elite revulsion. It was
the most significant catalyst of the Cold War, for it called
to mind the aggressions that had spawned World War II and
evoked memories of the dangers associated with appeasement.

Major policies such as the Truman Doctrine and the creation
of the North Atlantic Treaty Organization (NATO) followed
from the prevailing perception that Soviet foreign policy
threatened vital national security interests. But these policies,
while major departures in their own right, fell short of the
military stance that was to become the cornerstone of the American approach to the Soviet Union. According to defense analyst
Fred Kaplan, 1949-50 was a turning point in the American approach to the Cold War.[16] In Kaplan's opinion, the decision
to engage America's resources in a global military confrontation
against communism derived from a combination of factors unfolding simultaneously at home and abroad. Internationally, the
fall of the Chinese mainland to Communist forces and the
Soviets' detonation of a nuclear device gave new and more
ominous immediacy to the Soviet specter. What gave these
events their definition at home was the changing constellation
of forces within the Truman administration. One of the major
constraints on defense spending prior to Truman's second
term was the predominance of fiscal conservatives among the
president's closest economic advisers. In 1949 a shakeup in
the Council of Economic Advisers gave Keynesian economics
a new life. Higher defense expenditures were now seen as consistent with a pump-priming philosophy. At the same time,
newly appointed Secretary of State Dean Acheson and policy
planner Paul Nitze—two officials with more or less hard-line
views on communism—managed to outmaneuver nonmilitarists

such as Kennan, Charles Bohlen, and Defense Secretary Louis Johnson to produce a controversial, interagency document, NSC-68, which among other things called for a dramatic increase in American military spending. While many within the government challenged the assumptions and conclusions of NSC-68, the outbreak of the Korean War led to its implementation and, in Kaplan's opinion, to its enshrinement as the bible of postwar American policy.

The concept of the national interest that evolved from the assumptions contained in NSC-68 identified the Soviet Union as the principal challenger to the nation's survival. The Soviets were perceived as menacing the very physical and political integrity of the state both through domestic ideological subversion and military extortion. Capitulation to such an enemy was seen as tantamount to national suicide. Soviet violations of self-determination and inspiration of Communist aggressions were considered antithetical to American principles of justice and democracy. Moreover, Soviet encroachments were seen as potentially upsetting to the bipolar balance of power by which America could insure its survival.

The anti-Communist component of the national interest was, however, constrained by the equally compelling threat of nuclear devastation. As early as 1945, the Truman administration forecast that the Soviets would eventually achieve a nuclear capability of their own. For this reason, Truman groped for a policy that could involve them in harnessing the dangerous potential of the atom. Domestic constraints and Truman's own skepticism about Soviet intentions eventually prevented the development of such a policy. Instead, the United States assumed that its temporary nuclear monopoly could be used to force Stalin into major concessions. That this approach failed suggests not only that the Soviets did not take the threat of nuclear attack seriously but also that hesitation at home about the uncertain consequences of a preventive nuclear strike was significant enough to make such an option politically and militarily unfeasible.

While the advent of a Soviet nuclear capability went a long way toward propelling the United States into a permanent warfare stance, it also forced strategists to consider modalities by which nuclear war could be averted. During Eisenhower's presidency, the doctrine of "brinkmanship," provocative as it was, was designed to avert the possibility that nuclear war should ever become a reality. Subsequent policies such as limited war, flexible response, arms control, and Richard Nixon's "linkage" doctrine, designed to offer positive inducements to the Soviets in return for their good behavior in a broad variety of areas, were similarly adopted to meet the conflicting requirements of anticommunism and nuclear war avoidance. As Seyom Brown wrote in his impressive book *The Faces of Power*, all these policies were linked by a common thread— that the pursuit of the national interest involved the attempt to avert having to choose between either of two fundamentally undesirable consequences: Communist advance and nuclear war.[17]

From this perspective it can be seen that the postwar stance of the United States was in no small part determined by factors over which policymakers had little control. The American commitment to democracy and the effort to preserve the physical and political integrity of the nation were inescapable components of the nation's international objectives. To be sure, American policymakers might have chosen a path of accommodation with the Soviet Union and resisted the development of a warfare state. The Soviets, however, showed little interest in satisfying even minimum American concerns. What is certainly true is that by the time the basic thrust of American Cold War policy evolved, the dimensions of the Soviet-American rivalry had already taken shape. Perceptions of the Soviet threat along with Soviet perceptions of the American threat were externalized to the point where the international system took on the character of those perceptions. Future policymakers were to be essentially hand-bound by the exigencies of that system.

What is most remarkable about this conception of the national interest is its resilience in the face of major global and strategic changes. Anticommunism is still the cornerstone of America's international stance, despite the evolution of the People's Republic of China into a putative anti-Soviet ally and the obvious disintegration of the global Communist movement. The United States, for example, continues to view most international situations, particularly internal wars, as contests between itself and the Soviets. Nuclear war avoidance has been an equally persistent imperative. The doctrine of deterrence developed at a time when the United States enjoyed clear nuclear superiority over the Soviets. It has survived the transition to nuclear parity and the

vicissitudes of the Soviet-American rivalry. Policy and strategic
adjustments have been made to conform to changing circumstances, but the basic outlines have remained the same.

One can therefore understand the strategic alternations in
American foreign policy as seeking to perpetuate certain core
features of the American national interest, the most prominent
being resistance to the Soviet military and political threat to the
nation. Nothing is more illustrative of the continuing importance
of this theme than the unfortunate experience of the Carter
administration. Jimmy Carter assumed the presidency at a time
when two developments called into question the validity of
the traditional Cold War response to Soviet communism. The
first of these developments was the Viet Nam debacle, which
challenged the utility of conventional military force in dealing
with the Communist threat. The second, more subtle development was the increasing importance of the north-south conflict
in international affairs. President Carter sought to meet the
Communist challenge by de-emphasizing the military aspects
of the American relationship with the Soviet Union. Instead,
he attempted to deprive the Soviets of opportunities for global
advance by seeking to stabilize underdeveloped areas where
conditions were conducive to Soviet penetration. The upshot
of these efforts was not only a weakening of domestic confidence in the president's ability to manage foreign affairs but
also a rude awakening for Carter when the Soviets invaded
Afghanistan in 1979. In response, the president reversed gears
dramatically and returned to a more traditional and militaristic
Cold War approach.

The Carter case presents a perfect example of the persistent
pressures of the international system on American foreign
policy. Carter came to the presidency without prior experience
in the Washington foreign policy establishment. Moreover,
as a presidential candidate Carter pledged himself to correct
the abuses of his Cold War predecessors. Infused with a profoundly
moralistic conception of world affairs, the new president sought
to move in novel directions. He muted the military dimension
of the Soviet-American confrontation in his approach to global
problems. He also—at least initially—rejected the contradictions
inherent in a policy that allowed for increased defense spending
even as arms control agreements were being negotiated and
concluded. Instead, Carter favored greater movement toward
disarmament, both at the negotiating table and in the formulation of defense policy.

But even a president as disposed toward moralism as Carter was ultimately forced to come to grips with the realities of the international system. A world order favorable to American interests in an era of protracted conflict could not be sustained in the absence of a rough equilibrium in military power between the superpowers. Nor could stability in that relationship be fostered through impressive but unrealizable proposals for disarmament. Both countries would have to proceed with incremental arms control measures, because those measures were most consistent with the inherent contradictions in U.S.-Soviet relations. Unfortunately for Carter, by the time he awakened to this reality, he had already alienated significant segments of his domestic and allied constituencies. For this reason, Carter's sudden shift appeared more a demonstration of inconsistency than anything else.

Ronald Reagan's accession to the presidency can be seen, in part, as a reaction to the perceived irresolution and weakness in Carter's foreign policy, although Carter's electoral defeat can be ascribed more to popular dissatisfaction with his domestic rather than foreign policies. In his first few months as president, Reagan flexed new muscle on the international scene by expanding defense appropriations during a time of otherwise shrinking federal budgetary outlays, by demonstrating greater support, both diplomatically and materially, for right-wing authoritarian regimes, and by launching rhetorical broadsides at the Soviet Union. Moreover, he appeared to turn his back on arms control by showing no great zeal to move his bureaucracy in the direction of an arms control policy, by appointing well-known opponents of SALT II to important disarmament posts, and by hinting that he might not be bound by previously negotiated agreements. To be sure, Reagan was not the first Cold War president to raise the military budget substantially; Kennedy presided over a large expansion in nuclear and conventional forces during the early 1960s. Nor was Reagan the first to inveigh against the Soviets; every president, to one degree or another, has engaged in anti-Soviet polemics. He was also not the first president to approach the question of arms control gingerly; Nixon tried to restrain his arms control bureaucracy from moving too quickly in 1969 so that he might induce the Soviets to collar their North Vietnamese allies in return for negotiations. What was unique about Reagan, however, was the relative uniformity of anti-Sovietism that showed through his initial policies. In other words, there appeared to be little deliberate effort on the part of the administration—apart perhaps from the domestically motivated repeal of the grain embargo—to leaven its anti-Soviet policies with accommodative gestures. Moreover, whereas skepticism about arms control in the 1950s' was in part the result of an uncertainty about its consequences, the reaction against arms control in the 1980s followed more than two decades of U.S.-Soviet negotiations and implied that there was a critical defect that rendered arms control inimical to the national interest.

Whether Reagan can sustain the initial thrust of these policies without seeking some accommodation with the Soviet Union, especially in the area of arms control, remains to be seen. Nuclear war avoidance has not diminished as a critical facet of the American national interest as even Reagan seemed to acknowledge near the end of his first year as president. For this reason, one can reasonably expect that when Reagan's rhetoric is tested by events where the available options are few and relatively narrow, the administration will, in practice, operate in a much more restrained fashion, as it did in response to the Polish crisis of December 1981. In addition, despite the president's own apparent skepticism about arms control, the pressure to negotiate with the Soviets will be strong. America's Western European allies have already forced the administration into negotiations over medium-range nuclear forces. Moreover, as the full force of budget cuts is felt in areas other than defense, it will become increasingly difficult for Reagan to defend a policy of a relatively unrestrained arms race. This is not to say that the administration will lose its anti-Communist character, but it does argue for a future policy that will be considerably more conventional and balanced in its treatment of the Soviet Union.

PRESIDENTS AND THE FOREIGN POLICY CONSENSUS

In responding to the conflicting pressures of the international system, a president does not operate free from internal constraint. He is bounded by imposing domestic political barriers composed of public opinion, the media, political parties, and interest groups. He can be frustrated by Congress, particularly with regard to bills and treaties requiring appropriation or ratification. Within the executive branch, he must often defer to bureaucratic considerations and organizational repertoires. In a very broad sense, he is limited by the prevailing foreign policy consensus that purports to define the national interest. Nevertheless, a president, operating within these parameters, performs a singular function that decisively affects the outcome of the foreign policy decision-making process, that is, the legitimization of policy that appears to violate the equilibrium between anticommunism and nuclear war avoidance.

The origins of the Cold War consensus can be traced to the period immediately following the close of World War II. Whereas President Truman initially hestitated to adopt a firm stance to deal with the Soviet problem, public opinion responded sharply to postwar Soviet behavior in Eastern Europe. In March 1946, only 7 percent of a nationwide Gallup sample approved of Soviet policies, and two months later 58 percent responded that the Soviets were attempting to rule the world.[18] Moreover, Congress and the Republican party, throughout 1945-46, were prodding the president toward a more resolute anti-Soviet posture. In 1945 Congress insisted that loans be granted to the Soviets only on condition that Truman extract meaningful concessions from them at the bargaining table. In early 1946, the Republican party threatened to tear apart years of wartime bipartisanship in response to Secretary of State James Byrne's somewhat autonomous and conciliatory overtures toward the Soviets. Truman himself appears to have been inclined toward a tougher stance, but domestic considerations, including a hotly contested congressional campaign, made the shift toward a decisive hard-line policy inevitable.

Opposition to alleged Soviet transgressions, no matter how ingrained in the public psyche, could not, however, be effectively implemented as long as the public refused to make the necessary sacrifices in the battle against communism. Soon after the war, public and congressional pressures led to a debilitating demobilization of the country's armed forces. Moreover, the 1946 elections produced a Republican majority in Congress, dominated by fiscal conservatives such as Robert Taft and Joseph Martin. For the administration to secure funds for propping up friendly regimes in Europe and the Mediterranean, the president would have to overcome those tendencies in the electorate and Congress that did not correspond to the requirements of an internationalist foreign policy.

The Truman Doctrine and Marshall Plan will long be remembered for thrusting the United States into an active policy of containment against the Soviet Union. But no less significant was the influence that the rhetoric attached to these policies was to have in creating the ideological rationale for the Cold War. In his address to Congress in March 1947 Truman stressed that the battle between the United States and Soviet Union

was a global confrontation between two antithetical ideologies—
totalitarianism versus freedom. The president explained that
the Truman Doctrine committed the United States to the universal defense of the latter. In actuality the administration
harbored few illusions about the extent to which the United
States was prepared to roll back communism. Truman stopped
short of demanding military mobilization and in the case of
China two years later, did not step in to arrest the Communist
takeover. Nevertheless, Truman presented his case in a manner
designed to arouse the public to the nature of the threat facing
the nation. Dramatically oversimplified as his speech was, it
nevertheless had the desired effect of making anticommunism
the touchstone of postwar American foreign policy. It is not
surprising, therefore, that by March 1948, a plurality of respondents to a Gallup Poll agreed with the proposition that the
United States should be prepared to fight the Soviet Union or
that by late 1949 the Survey Research Center should report
that there existed an almost unanimous belief that the Soviet
Union was an aggressive, expansion-minded nation. The Korean
War and the rearmament program that it engendered were ultimately to lock the United States into a rigid Cold War perception of the Soviet Union and international communism and
institutionalize the military component in American foreign
policy.

As already noted, the evolution of the Cold War was not
preordained. Instead, the perceptions of the key actors on both
sides tended to define the dimensions and intensity of U.S.-
Soviet competition. The bipolar system that emerged subsequently developed an autonomous, inertial quality that
compelled both parties to conform to its dictates. The same
may be said for the domestic system in the United States.
While the perceptions of policymakers were substantially more
sophisticated than those of the electorate, the essentially
Manichean cast by which Truman and his associates rationalized
the Cold War sharpened and rigidified the anti-Soviet tendencies
in the general public.[19] Once set in motion, these attitudes
were to become even more confining to policymakers than the
international system that helped to mold them.

Continuing rigidities in the American approach to the Soviet
Union in the period following the evolution of the Cold War
can be attributed to a number of factors. First, the threat posed
by the Soviet Union did not appreciably diminish during the
1950s and 1960s. Whereas the death of Stalin promised new

direction in the course of Soviet policy, the Soviets' increasing strategic power coupled with the bellicosity of Stalin's immediate successors offered what appeared to be even more imposing threats to the national interest. Second, the generation of policymakers who engineered American foreign policy during the first twenty-five years of the Cold War—from Truman through Nixon—were historically conditioned by the experiences that had led to World War II. For these policymakers, most notably Lyndon Johnson in his handling of the Viet Nam War, appeasement was an unparalleled evil that had to be avoided with resolute firmness.[20] Finally, the public view of the Soviet Union that emerged in response to postwar Soviet behavior was dogmatically anti-Communist. This rather superficial portrait of the Soviet threat was antithetical to the appreciation of sophisticated nuances in the nature and evolution of communism. Policymakers were, therefore, constrained from taking advantage of potentially positive changes in Soviet behavior without simultaneously proving their anti-Communist mettle.

The constraint of anticommunism, however, was not as paralyzing in its impact on policy as was, for example, the isolationism of the 1920s and 1930s. According to Gabriel Almond, public opinion in the 1940s and 1950s could be seen as essentially permissive, willing to follow the lead of a resolute elite.[21] This permissiveness can be attributed to the ambivalent nature of the national interest. Whereas the public supported the development of a large military complex to meet the Communist threat, it was not at all indifferent to the prospects of nuclear war.[22] During the 1950s, as nuclear warfare evolved into an ominous and ubiquitous threat to national survival, the public accorded guarded support to prospects for possible coexistence with the enemy. Almond, writing in 1960, commented, "There is a widespread sense of personal and national vulnerability to modern instruments of destruction."[23] This anxiety, coupled with the public's determination to arrest Communist expansion, led Ralph Levering to write that during the Eisenhower and Kennedy years, "The public generally wanted to contain communism, but also wanted to keep out of war."[24]

Nuclear war avoidance and anticommunism set the outermost boundaries and the terms of foreign policy debate for the Cold War. Whereas both goals were accepted as the essential ingredients of the national interest, the distance between them was substantial enough to produce intense controversy over specific foreign policy measures. No issue in Soviet-American relations is more illustrative of this fact than the problem of arms control. Whereas arms control recognizes the perhaps permanent existence of intense military and political competition between the United States and U.S.S.R., it also assumes that both sides have a mutual interest in averting the cataclysmic consequences of nuclear war. As an issue, therefore, arms control both substantively and symbolically reflects the conflicting demands of the bipolar international system and the ambivalent nature of the American national interest. In formulating arms control policy, decision makers are driven to seek a balance between the objectives of nuclear war avoidance and anticommunism. Any policy that veers too far toward one side or the other is seen as threatening the delicate equilibrium that maintains America's survival in the face of the twin threats of nuclear war and Soviet communism.

The difficulty of achieving such a fine balance derives most prominently from uncertainty regarding the enemy's capabilities and intentions. Complicating the task, however, are different assessments among the attentive public and policy-making elite in the United States regarding the utility of arms control as it relates to the national interest. Robert Levine in his still-useful book *The Arms Debate*, published in 1963, divided the spectrum of opinion on this issue into five schools of thought.[25] Two of the schools—antiwar and anticommunist systemists—fall outside the national foreign policy consensus—the former because they do not see in relation to their own antiwar ideology any equally compelling threat from communism, and the latter because they do not see in relation to their own anti-Communist, ideology any equally compelling threat from nuclear war. While these schools have some impact on the arms control debate, their actual influence on policy is marginal. The mainstream schools, labeled "marginalist," define the national interest as constituting avoidance of both Communist encroachments and nuclear war. Nevertheless, within the mainstream there are significant differences of opinion. Antiwar marginalists believe that the Soviet Union poses a great danger to the United States but oppose policies that, in seeking to stop the Soviets, create undue risks of nuclear war. This group generally favors reductions in defense spending and more ambitious disarmament initiatives while resisting military interventions abroad. Anti-Communist marginalists do not propose to initiate a nuclear war against the U.S.S.R. but feel that arms control agreements work to the advantage of the Kremlin, who are fundamentally untrustworthy.

They generally favor unilateral expansion in defense expenditures as a method by which deterrence can be strengthened. Middle marginalists borrow from the concerns of both schools and tend to rely strongly on measures such as mutual deterrence, limited war, and arms control negotiations.

Policy formulation toward the Soviet Union can be understood as reflecting the movement of a pendulum that never quite reaches its extremities but rather hovers uneasily in the middle range of its arc. During the 1950s, the pendulum veered toward the anti-Communist marginalists, not in the sense of provoking war with the Soviet Union but in terms of a general avoidance of serious negotiations with the Kremlin. By the late 1950s, intramural debate within the Eisenhower administration along with increased agitation in Congress and among the attentive public in favor of a nuclear test ban moved Eisenhower toward negotiations. The Kennedy and Johnson administrations, on the other hand, were authentically middle marginal in the sense that both pursued negotiations while increasing defense budgets and prosecuting the war in Viet Nam. This approach was tempered, particularly in relation to arms control, by the prevailing mood of anticommunism—which the war did little to attentuate—but the ambivalences that characterized their policies were fairly consistent with a national consensus that defined security as a balance between anticommunism and nuclear war avoidance.

The Nixon administration is generally credited with engineering the policy of détente, although the basic elements of détente existed as early as the Eisenhower administration and continued through the administrations of his immediate Democratic successors. During Nixon's tenure in office active United States military involvement in Viet Nam came to a close, the so-called "Nixon Doctrine," which urged America's allies not to rely exclusively on American troop involvement in their behalf, emerged and the superpowers agreed to limit and negotiate future ceilings on strategic nuclear weapons. In addition, Washington and Moscow established a pattern of summit diplomacy de- to foster better relations across a whole range of contentious political issues in line with the administration's commitment to a policy of "linkage." The Nixon foreign policy could thus be described as middle marginal. Nevertheless, under Nixon, and for the first time since the promulgation of NSC-68, an administration was forced to grapple with a significant challenge from the proponents of antiwar marginalism. The emergence

of a strong antiwar marginalist position in the early 1970s was
to tip the pendulum in a way that was significantly, albeit incre-
mentally, at variance with the prior direction of postwar American foreign policy.

The breakdown of the middle-marginal consensus that had
guided policymakers throughout the late 1950s and 1960s can
of course be attributed to the debilitating war in Indochina.
Not only did the failure of that war call into question the
utility of military force as an instrument of American foreign
policy, but it also, in conjunction with anxiety over domestic
disorder at home, generated a flagging of U.S. determination
to bear the burden of containment abroad. Moreover, years of
détente, beginning with the 1963 Nuclear Test Ban Treaty,
along with the obvious corrosion of the Communist bloc, raised
new questions about the severity of the Soviet threat. Nixon
and his national security adviser Henry Kissinger recognized
that the changing nature of the Communist world offered opportunities for policy departures, but they did not subscribe to a
benign view of the Soviet Union and international communism.
Instead, they hoped to offer the Soviets a mixture of carrots
and sticks in return for accommodation. The implementation
of their policies was, however, at least in Kissinger's and Nixon's
views, threatened by the rising tide of antiwar sentiment on
Capitol Hill. Much of this sentiment focused on congressional
efforts to bring an early end to the war in Viet Nam. Nixon
and Kissinger agreed that the war had to end, but they were
convinced that a precipitate withdrawal of forces from Viet
Nam would undermine the U.S. stance vis-à-vis the Soviet Union.
The president outmaneuvered his opponents by undertaking
unilateral military actions while Vietnamizing the war effort.
Perhaps most frustrating to Nixon and Kissinger, however, was
Congress's alleged attempt to impose unilateral restraints on
defense spending.[26] Nixon and Kissinger believed that the
Soviets could be induced to make strategic concessions only
if the U.S. could bargain from a position of strength. Thus the
administration felt strongly that to secure an antiballistic
missile (ABM) agreement, the United States would first have
to deploy an ABM of its own; to gain concessions on strategic
weapons, the U.S. would have to add the multiple independently
targetable reentry vehicle (MIRV) to its own force. According
to Kissinger, the American negotiating stance was seriously im-
paired by the need to satisfy the antidefense sentiment in
Washington—a sentiment that Nixon felt the administration had

to respond to if it was to leave its mark on American foreign policy.

The Nixon experience, in retrospect, was unlike those of his immediate predecessors, Kennedy and Johnson, even though his policy orientation was not significantly different from theirs. Kennedy and Johnson operated within an environment that was strongly anti-Communist. In moving toward limited accommodation with the Kremlin, both presidents were vulnerable to attack from anti-Communist marginalists and consequently had to move gingerly on questions such as arms control. Nixon's strong anti-Communist credentials essentially neutralized the political right wing, although he did experience marginal difficulties with some conservative members of his party and more serious ones with defense-minded Democrats such as Senator Henry Jackson. By far, Nixon's greatest difficulty, however, stemmed from the fact that he entered the White House at a time when the nation's anti-Communist ardor was going into temporary remission. While this allowed Nixon to pursue arms control with great domestic success, it also made it difficult for the president to pursue détente in the hard-line manner he preferred. The unraveling of the Nixon presidency and the political weakness of his successor, Gerald Ford, veered the nation toward a tentative antiwar marginalist course. This could be attributed to two factors. First, the presidency, which had evolved in the 1950s and 1960s into the anchor of middle marginalism, was seriously weakened in relation to Congress, where the antiwar marginalists were strongest. Second, the failure of the means traditionally associated with middle marginalism created a sense of irresolution—not unlike the one that immediately followed the close of World War II—that no president was yet strong enough to overcome.

The Carter election and the first few years of his presidency can be understood as a short-lived victory for an ill-defined antiwar marginalism. Carter's campaign called for reductions in defense spending and the avoidance of Viet Nam-like involvements abroad. As president, Carter proposed to the Soviets "deep cuts" in armaments and de-emphasized the military character of containment. But the advent of the Carter presidency also dovetailed with a renewal of an anti-Communist mood in the mass and attentive public. Carter's reluctance or inability to respond with military assistance to alleged Soviet-inspired aggressions in the horn of Africa or to major revolutionary changes in other parts of the world sharpened this mood. Controversial presidential decisions such as the cancellation of the B-1 bomber, suspension of the neutron bomb, and promotion of the Panama Canal Treaties contributed to strengthening the hands of the anti-Communists. The results of this swing in the opinion pendulum were twofold. First, it became impossible for Carter to win support for the SALT II Treaty. A constellation of groups, labeled by foreign policy specialist Dimitri Simes as "the Anti-Soviet Brigade," joined forces to fight against ratification of the agreement.[27] Because Carter was vulnerable to the charge that he was "soft" on communism, it was next to impossible for him to portray the treaty as promoting the national interest. Second, whether for political or ideological reasons, the president found it necessary to abandon the antiwar marginalist position and to move dramatically to the right. This change of direction included temporary suspension of the SALT II ratification process, increased defense spending, renewed draft registration, the establishment of a quick-strike mobile expeditionary force, the adoption of a limited war nuclear strategy, and the suspension of ongoing negotiations with the Soviet Union. In four years, the pendulum had swung to the anti-Communist segment of the policy spectrum, a swing that saw ultimate confirmation in Reagan's election victory.

The marginalist consensus can be understood as deriving from two fundamental foreign policy objectives—anti-communism and nuclear war avoidance. Within this broad consensus, there are competing policy orientations. At times, the domestic balance of forces between these tendencies is in equilibrium. At other times, either antiwar or anti-Communist marginalism is dominant. Postwar presidents have generally been middle marginalists, in part because the foreign policy establishment from which presidents draw their closest advisers has traditionally been dominated by middle marginalists. But there is another, even more important reason for the middle marginalism of presidents: No matter their individual policy orientation, they must satisfy the conflicting strains of informed public opinion. For this reason, Kennedy felt that to achieve a test ban treaty with the Soviet Union, he had to increase military spending and authorize an accelerated underground testing program. Nixon reasoned that to achieve support for his firm policy of détente, he would have to end the war in Viet Nam and achieve cuts in defense spending. Carter, more antiwar marginalist than any other president, ultimately agreed in anticipation of a Senate battle over SALT II to authorize an MX missile program and

to enhance the American military posture, even before the
Soviet invasion of Afghanistan.

In all of these cases, the management of the inherent contradictions in the American national interest and conflicting
impulses in public opinion fell to the president. Arms control,
in particular, involves not only strategic decisions but domestic
political calculations as well. In essence, arms control requires
an evaluation on the part of an administration regarding the
extent of superpower collaboration allowable within the
boundaries of political opinion at home. Inevitably, the one
political figure who can calibrate these limits is a president;
first because he, as opposed to his bureaucracy, is politically
accountable to domestic opinion, and second because he and
no other governmental actor can reach such a large constituency
with so authoritative a voice. Consequently, arms control policy
is either constrained or enhanced by a president's calculation
of the extent to which he is able to commit his powers to legitimize specific measures as consistent with the national interest.

President Kennedy was able to work successfully toward a
limited détente because he was operating within a well-defined
consensus, was cautious enough to understand the limits of
that consensus, and was enough of a political mobilizer to pro-
mote his policies as being consistent with that consensus.
President Nixon was successful first because his past secured him
against assault from the right and second because his secretive,
dramatic method of decision making outmaneuvered his opponents on the left. Nonetheless, the Nixon presidency saw the
beginnings of a decline in the middle marginal consensus that
had guided both him and his predecessors. His successors, Ford
and most notably Carter, suffered in comparison not so much
from their own ineptitude as from the absence of a firm foreign
policy consensus that could give them direction. Coupled with
the enervation of institutional prestige that Watergate inflicted
on the presidency, the erosion of any firm middle marginal
constituency and the swelling of the extremes made Carter's
floundering symptomatic of a deeper malaise—the disintegration of a national foreign policy consensus.

It is too early to judge whether Reagan's decided tilt toward
the anti-Communist portion of the political spectrum is symptomatic of a new consensus that is substantially different from
the one that guided the country in the 1960s and 1970s.
Opinion data from the 1980 campaign suggest that the public
is still terribly anxious about the prospects of nuclear war. It

remains to be seen whether Reagan can generate over the long run the necessary support to sustain in the face of the inevitable internal and external stresses a policy of confrontation and increased defense spending. The lesson of his predecessor suggests that a president who moves too far in one direction or the other will either dissipate his support or find himself forced into the middle.

PRESIDENTS, BUREAUCRATS, AND SOVIET-AMERICAN RELATIONS

In recent years scholarly attention has concentrated on the central role of government agencies in the formulation of foreign policy. Most noteworthy in this regard is Graham Allison's *Essence of Decision*, which offered two variations of the bureaucratic model to explain foreign policy decision making—the organizational process and governmental politics paradigms.[28] The former, which borrows heavily from the literature on organizational behavior, sees foreign policy as an aggregated outcome of disjointed bureaucratic decisions, each in turn traceable to standard operating procedures and repertoires. The latter, which relies on the works of political scientists such as Richard Neustadt, Samuel Huntington, and Charles Lindblom, views foreign policy as a political result in which the central actors are government agencies. Organizational stands are determined by a mixture of motives including personal goals, bureaucratic interests, and policy orientations. A wide body of scholarly writing has since developed to expand on the basic premises that Allison offered some ten years ago.

While there are significant differences between these two approaches, they tend to converge on certain basic conclusions. First, according to bureaucratic scholars, the key locus of decision-making power lies in government organizations, not in the wider political system. Thus, policy making can best be understood by concentrating on intramural debate within the executive branch. Second, foreign policy cannot be viewed as a rational and purposive application of the national interest. Instead, strategies are chosen either because they conform to preexisting routines or because they manage to satisfy the widest range of bureaucratic interests. Third, policy making tends to be incremental, not because the national interest is necessarily stable, but because bureaucratic movement is invariably inertial. Fourth, the lack of uniformity and consistency in the nation's foreign policy is attributable to the fragmentation of the decision-making process rather than to any centrally orchestrated ambivalence. Finally, the role of the president in the policy-making process is less than decisive and often anticlimactic. Whereas bureaucratic scholars are somewhat ambivalent in their treatment of presidential power, it is safe to say that I. M. Destler is fairly representative when he wrote:

> There are considerable grounds for believing, then, that to treat United States foreign policy as the direct outcome of decisions made by the President is to distort the process considerably. Instead, one might better begin by characterizing United States foreign policy as the outcome of a stream of decisions and actions taken by officials in a range of agencies and at several bureaucratic levels.[29]

The constraining influence of bureaucracy that scholars such as Allison and Destler noted is indeed strong. Especially in the case of Soviet-American relations, where a broad spectrum of issues is involved, the constellation of participating actors, including presidents, is both large and variable from one area to the next. Thus, whereas one issue might bear the imprint of a particular agency, another might be affected more greatly by some other agency. During the Eisenhower administration, for example, defense policy was influenced prominently by the secretary of the treasury, whereas arms control policy was affected by representatives of the Atomic Energy Commission, the State Department, and the president's science adviser. Nevertheless, just as different issues mobilize a variety of bureaucratic actors, so too a certain class of issues demands a higher level of presidential attention. To be sure, the probability that a president will involve himself in a particular issue depends, in large part, on the individual president's proclivity. But it also depends on the nature of the issue itself. Issues that so divide the executive branch that they require presidential intervention fit this category. Moreover, issues that mobilize political concerns in the broader arena invariably force the president to intervene, if only to protect the chief executive's status as a national leader.

Probably no issue pertaining to Soviet-American relations arouses greater bureaucratic controversy about national security than arms control. Here, presidential leadership is crucial, not only in legitimizing policies as consistent with the national interest, but also in integrating policy choices in an area where centrifugal bureaucratic tendencies are so strong. The fragmented character of decision making in this area is related to three factors. First, arms control, as an issue, involves the interests and the expertise of a large and varied group of government agencies. Second, it is the type of issue that has critical and direct bearing on organizational missions and assumptions about international politics. Consequently, it tends to produce high-intensity bureaucratic participation. Third, arms control is generally perceived by bureaucracies as a distributive issue whose outcome can seriously affect the allocation of resources within the government.

The policy problems that result from such a wide proliferation of interests and contending assumptions are obvious. Without significant centralization of command, the tendency to division can lead either to delays in the policy-making process, compromises that seriously dilute policy, or a failure to develop policy at all. The last alternative is highly unlikely, given the pressure placed on the policy-making system by bureaucratic groups in support of arms control, but delays and debilitating compromises are probable in the absence of any firm direction from the central policymaker and his chief subordinates.

Perhaps even more important in explaining the role of presidents in the arms control field is the need for an integrating theory that can fuse political and military considerations into a unified strategy. Arms control is sometimes viewed, even within the government, as concerned primarily with the negotiation of agreements to limit the arms race. In this sense, it is often perceived, particularly by the military, as isolated from and even antithetical to the development of a strong strategic posture. Arms control, however, is a policy that recognizes the existence of a Soviet-American interest in averting general war, either through avoidance or through the limitation of war once it has erupted. Consequently, a policy of arms control involves not only the negotiation of treaties to limit the level or character of armaments on both sides but also the development of a military strategy that, either unilaterally or through reciprocation, attempts to stabilize deterrence.

The proclivity of government organizations to compartmentalize military and arms control considerations results from the notion that the two areas rest on vastly differing assumptions about Soviet behavior. Arms control policy has involved the belief that the superpowers have a joint interest in limiting the possibilities of nuclear war. Traditionally, military strategy has been based on the assumption that the objectives of the two great nuclear powers are incompatible. A policy of arms control, however, recognizes, first, that the retention of military power is crucial to the stability of the balance of terror and, second, that military strategy can also be developed on the basis of a shared interest between the United States and the Soviet Union. Whereas "disarmament" assumes that war is prevented by the "eradication of military establishments, military tradition, and military thinking,"[30] arms control assumes that war is prevented by some kind of deterrence. This means that each side, rather than abolish or drastically reduce its military forces, will develop a force that places a premium on the avoidance or limitation of nuclear war.

Political centralization is necessary to overcome the centrifugal bureaucratic tendencies militating against the assimilation of specific measures to curb the arms race with an overall strategic posture. Resistance to such integration is strong, in part because a strategic posture guided by arms control considerations does not necessarily lead to an increase in the military budget. Perhaps more importantly, arms control requires that all elements of the executive branch recognize the inherent interest of the superpowers in some form of military collaboration, political differences notwithstanding. This requires strong central direction, presumably from a secretary of defense but more importantly from a president himself. Organizations often accentuate those policies that are most closely related to their respective missions. Thus, the military focuses on defending the state against its enemies, while the disarmament experts press for a reduction in weapons. In doing so, each group tends to lose sight of the broader picture. It is, therefore, a president's responsibility to maintain the balance between policies aimed at frustrating Soviet power objectives and those aimed at seeking some accommodation between the two sides.

An example of the president's role in overcoming the fissional tendencies of the bureaucracy is provided by Lyndon Johnson's decision in 1967 to fund development of an ABM system.[31] The ABM issue contained both strategic and arms control dimensions. To its proponents, the ABM promised defense against a first-strike nuclear attack. To its detractors, however, the ABM threatened to undermine the delicate balance of mutual deterrence existing between the superpowers. Within the administration, the forces in favor of the ABM were led by the Joint Chiefs of Staff, who had considerable support on Capitol Hill. Those opposed were led by Secretary of Defense Robert McNamara, by then increasingly restive over the president's Viet Nam policy.

Johnson's decision to go ahead with funding for the ABM reflected his sensitivity to congressional and military pressures, but the manner in which the decision was implemented can be traced to the president's desire to salvage a hoped-for arms accord with the Soviet Union. Johnson instructed McNamara to announce the ABM decision. In his speech, the secretary was permitted to couple his announcement with an attack against the argument that the ABM could possibly provide a credible defense against Soviet missiles. On the contrary, argued McNamara, an anti-Soviet ABM would only induce the Soviets to build more offensive weapons. Instead, according to the secretary of defense, the ABM as contemplated was designed to defend against the relatively modest Chinese nuclear force. While Johnson allowed McNamara to make an essentially anti-ABM speech, he also permitted the Joint Chiefs of Staff to defend the ABM in terms of its potential to thwart a Soviet attack.

Clearly, Johnson tried to placate those in his administration and in Congress who favored the ABM as an anti-Soviet measure. In doing so, however, the president also attempted to give the ABM decision a decided arms control cast. By announcing a decision to fund rather than deploy, Johnson was providing the Soviets with an opportunity to respond with concessions of their own ABM. Moreover, the president simultaneously authorized the State Department to initiate talks with the Soviets on the limitation of strategic arms. The failure of the Soviets to respond affirmatively to these initiatives, not unexpected given the tortured reasoning behind the American decision, along with McNamara's resignation in late 1967, led the president to a decision to deploy the ABM in early 1968. But Johnson saw this decision as providing the United States with a bargaining chip that could be used to negotiate future limitations on a Soviet ABM. Thus, President Johnson's decisions about the ABM in 1967-68 were essentially designed to reconcile opposing bureaucratic positions and at the same time to give impetus to arms control negotiations.

The nature of policy making, particularly in an area so dependent on expertise as arms control, demands the inclusion of certain bureaucratic groups in the decision-making process. Furthermore, the opposition of bureaucracy to presidential policies can have serious consequences in undermining the president's ability to marshall support in the political system at large. In 1976, for example, President Ford decided not to press for a SALT II accord that Kissinger favored because Secretary of Defense Donald Rumsfeld and the Joint Chiefs of Staff were opposed to provisions linking the American cruise missile to the Soviet backfire bomber. The president calculated that in an election year, with a major conservative challenge from his own party threatening his renomination, he could not possibly buck bureaucratic opposition of this kind.[32]

The extent of a president's control is, in large part, a consequence of the patterns of intragovernmental interaction which a president institutionalizes. All presidents have distinctive management styles, some more successful than others. But in specific cases, control is a function of four variables. First, what is the extent of personal presidential involvement? Presidents must choose those areas where they are willing to expend maximum attention, time, and prestige. The more a president involves himself directly in specific decision-making areas, the more control he asserts over government output, although in doing so he might minimize his influence in other areas. President Carter, for example, became extremely knowledgeable in the details of the SALT II negotiating process and hence could intervene in numerous cases where the arms controllers, such as Paul Warnke and Cyrus Vance, found themselves at odds with relative hard-liners such as National Security Adviser Zbigniew Brzezinski, the Joint Chiefs of Staff, and occasionally, Defense Secretary Harold Brown.[33] Second, presidents orchestrate the scope and character of bureaucratic involvement in specific issue areas. While this power is constrained by the need for organizational expertise, presidents can limit the flow of information to specific groups and establish ad hoc or new organizational arrangements in areas where they seek to circumvent conventional decision-making processes. Carter's ill-fated decision in March 1977 to propose to the Soviets "deep cuts" in strategic arms was made at a "principals only" meeting, and followed by the president's admonition to Secretary of State Cyrus Vance not to divulge details of the proposals even to his own staff on his mission to Moscow. While such an approach can easily demoralize a bureaucratic group, it can be effective when used with discretion.

Third, the president is the person who staffs his administration at the highest levels and who can, under certain circumstances, dismiss obstinate officials. In 1975, for example, President Ford found himself increasingly at odds with Secretary of Defense James Schlesinger, who was simultaneously at loggerheads with Secretary of State Kissinger.[34] Ford was inclined to favor Kissinger's approach toward the Soviet Union and arms control, whereas Schlesinger, who fashioned himself a hard-liner on national security issues, leaked comments critical of the administration's policies to the press. In relation to arms control, Schlesinger and the Joint Chiefs of Staff opposed Kissinger's apparent readiness to strike a deal on the American cruise missile. Ironically, in the early 1970s, the Defense Department had attempted to scuttle the cruise only to be overriden by Kissinger, who believed that the weapon could be used as a bargaining chip. In the mid-1970s, however, while Kissinger was inclined to make trade-offs involving cruise, the Defense Department was adamantly opposed to any such concessions. Ford ultimately stepped in to dismiss Schlesinger and thereby secured Kissinger's preeminent status in the administration's foreign policy hierarchy.

Finally, presidents retain the ability to undertake dramatic foreign policy initiatives either against the advice of their bureaucracy or without the knowledge of specific organizations. A classic example of this style is Nixon's handling of the bureaucracy. In contrast to Carter, Nixon was bored by the details of arms control negotiations but had a trusted and highly competent national security adviser in Henry Kissinger, who was exceedingly adept at manipulating the government's national security apparatus. At times Nixon and Kissinger deferred to their arms control bureaucracy, as they did in early 1969 when they agreed to convene the first Strategic Arms Limitation Treaty (SALT I) negotiations earlier than they preferred. But as time went on, the president and his lieutenant managed to dominate the negotiating process by establishing a secret "back channel" linking Kissinger to Soviet Ambassador Anatoly Dobrynin. There were several reasons for this approach.[35] First, Nixon and Kissinger were wary of the arms control proponents and their alleged tendency to seek concessions through unilateral restraint. Second, the president and his national security adviser were extremely sensitive to leaks. They hoped to plug holes in the national security machinery by restricting the flow of information to the negotiators in Helsinki and Vienna. Finally, the formal SALT policy-making machinery

was too slow and cumbersome to suit the president and
Kissinger. Instead, they preferred a decision-making process
that gave the appearance of interagency consultations but
through secretiveness avoided the pitfalls of bureaucratic consensus-building. Thus, Nixon, who experienced many frustra-
tions with his foreign policy bureaucracy, managed, at least in
the case of SALT I, to make himself temporary master over the
policy-making process.

The bureaucratic model is useful in illuminating the nature
of decision making in the foreign policy field. Nevertheless, in
accepting its observations about the complexities of policy
making, one need not embrace the assumptions and conclusions
about the centrality of bureaucratic power that are generally
associated with the organizational approach. Particularly in the
case of Soviet-American relations, there is sufficient evidence
to indicate that whereas bureaucracies are critical actors in
policy formulation and implementation, more traditional
approaches to foreign policy analysis that focus on international systems and presidential leadership are equally instructive. In its broadest sense, American foreign policy toward the
Soviet Union since the end of World War II can be seen as
highly rational and purposive, regardless of its apparent ambivalences. Successive presidents have retained the broad outlines
of policy toward the Soviets as defined by an ambiguous national interest. This continuity can be attributed to the persistence of the Soviet threat and the inexorable pressures of
the ongoing balance of terror. Moreover, whereas policy details
have invariably been shaped by bureaucratic considerations, the
most important areas of the superpower relationship, including
arms control, have been equally affected by domestic political
calculations. In these cases, the president's role has been para-
mount, not only in the formulation, but more importantly,
in the legitimization of policies. Thus, the ambivalent
nature of American foreign policy is not just a function of
the fragmented character of bureaucratic decision making.
Instead, it is a function of deliberate presidential efforts to maintain an objective if ambiguous national interest and at the same
time satisfy the mosaic of opinions that compose the American
foreign policy consensus.

NOTES

1. Paul Seabury, *The Rise and Decline of the Cold War* (New York
and London: Basic Books, 1967), p. 11.
2. Ibid., p. 13.

3. Edmund Morris, *The Rise of Theodore Roosevelt* (New York: Coward, McCann and Geoghegan, 1979), p. 572.

4. Richard Nixon, *The Memoirs of Richard Nixon*, vol. 1 (New York: Warner Books, 1978), p. 426.

5. Franz Schurmann, *The Logic of World Order* (New York: Random House, 1974).

6. J. David Singer, "The Level of Analysis Problem in International Relations," in *The International System: Theoretical Essays*, ed. Klaus Knorr and Sidney Verba (Princeton, N.J.: Princeton University Press, 1961), pp. 77-92.

7. Wolfram F. Hanrieder, "Actor Objectives and International Systems," in *Comparative Foreign Policy: Theoretical Essays*, ed. Hanrieder (New York: David McKay Company, Inc., 1971), pp. 108-31.

8. Ibid., p. 111.

9. Ibid.

10. Arnold Wolfers, "The Actors in International Politics," in *The Theory and Practice of International Relations*, ed. Fred A. Sondermann, David S. McLellan, and William C. Olson (Englewood Cliffs, N.J.: Prentice-Hall, 1979), pp. 12-13.

11. Seyom Brown, *The Faces of Power* (New York and London: Columbia University Press, 1968), p. 8.

12. Wolfers, "The Actors," p. 13.

13. Paul Y. Hammond, *Cold War and Detente: The American Foreign Policy Process Since 1945* (New York: Harcourt, Brace, Jovanovich, 1975), p. 37.

14. Daniel Yergin, *Shattered Peace: The Origins of the Cold War and the National Security State* (Boston: Houghton Mifflin, 1977).

15. John Gaddis, *The United States and the Origins of the Cold War, 1941-1947* (New York and London: Columbia University Press, 1972), p. 17.

16. Fred Kaplan, "Our Cold War Policy, Circa '50," *The New York Times Magazine*, 18 May 1980, pp. 34, 88-94.

17. Brown, *Faces of Power*, p. 8.

18. Ralph B. Levering, *The Public and American Foreign Policy, 1918-1978* (New York: William Morrow and Co., 1978), p. 97.

19. Cecil V. Crabb, Jr., *Policy-Makers and Critics: Conflicting Theories of American Foreign Policy* (New York: Praeger, 1976), pp. 90-91.

20. See Michael Roskin, "From Pearl Harbor to Vietnam: Shifting Generational Paradigms and Foreign Policy," *Political Science Quarterly* 89 (Fall 1974): 563-88.

21. Gabriel A. Almond, *The American People and Foreign Policy* (New York: Praeger, 1960), p. 88.

22. Ibid., pp. 114-15.

23. Ibid., p. xxxiii.

24. Levering, *The Public and Foreign Policy*, p. 116.

25. Robert A. Levine, *The Arms Debate* (Cambridge, Mass.: Harvard University Press, 1963).

26. Henry Kissinger, *White House Years* (Boston: Little, Brown, 1979), p. 535.

27. Dimitri K. Simes, "The Anti-Soviet Brigade," *Foreign Policy* 37 (Winter 1979-80): 28-42.

28. Graham Allison, *Essence of Decision* (Boston: Little, Brown, 1971); idem, "Conceptual Models and the Cuban Missile Crisis," *The American Political Science Review* 65 (September 1969): 689-718.

29. I. M. Destler, "Comment: Multiple Advocacy: Some 'Limits and Costs'," *The American Political Science Review* 66 (September 1972): 788.

30. See Thomas C. Schelling and Morton H. Halperin, *Strategy and Arms Control* (New York: The Twentieth Century Fund, 1961), p. 143.

31. Lyndon Baines Johnson, *The Vantage Point: Perspectives of the Presidency 1963-1969* (New York: Holt, Rinehart and Winston, 1971), pp. 479-81; Morton H. Halperin, *Bureaucratic Politics and Foreign Policy* (Washington, D.C.: Brookings Institution, 1974).

32. Gerald R. Ford, *A Time to Heal: The Autobiography of Gerald R. Ford* (New York: Harper and Row, 1979), p. 357.

33. For an excellent journalistic account of the SALT II negotiating process, see Strobe Talbot, *Endgame* (New York: Harper and Row, 1979).

34. Ford, *A Time to Heal*, pp. 320-26.

35. Kissinger, *White House Years*, pp. 1216-17.

2.
THE DÉTENTE OF 1963

The year 1963 was marked by an apparent departure from the
patterns of Soviet-American interaction that had evolved in
the aftermath of World War II. In August, representatives of
the United States, Soviet Union, and United Kingdom, agreeing to shelve a more politically vexatious pact banning underground nuclear testing, initialed a treaty prohibiting the
detonation of nuclear explosions in the air, sea, and outerspace;
thereby ending a seventeen-year negotiating impasse that had
begun with the collapse of the Baruch Plan, the Truman administration's proposal for the international sharing of nuclear
energy. Almost as a prelude to the test ban, American and Soviet
negotiators agreed in principle in April to the establishment of
a direct communications link between their two capitals; two
months later, the "hot line" became a reality.

On June 10, President John F. Kennedy delivered a major
foreign policy address calling on the American people to reevaluate their attitudes toward the Soviet Union and indicating
areas that were of mutual interest to the superpowers. Later
that year, shortly after Senate ratification of the Test Ban
Treaty, the president approved the sale of surplus wheat by
private American concerns to the Soviet Union, thus signaling
a change in the highly restrictive American approach to East-
West trade. By mid-October, bilateral negotiations were either
progressing or contemplated to initiate direct air service between
New York and Moscow, open new consulates in both countries,
settle the Soviet war debt, establish a joint communications
satellite system, and engage in a combined space program.

The notion that Soviet-American relations were moving in

new directions was acknowledged at the time by informed segments of the American public. As a reaction to the successful conclusion of the Moscow talks, the mass circulation periodical *Newsweek* titled its August 5 issue "A Truce in the Cold War?"[1] Later that year, in response to Senate ratification of the Test Ban Treaty, the highly respected *Bulletin of Atomic Scientists* set back its "death watch"—an imaginary clock signaling the approach of nuclear disaster—from 11:52 to 11:48.[2] While others, opposed to or chary about these developments, warned of the dangers inherent in peace "euphoria,"[3] it is clear that among the attentive public there was a realization that Soviet-American relations, for either good or bad, were entering a new phase.

The appearance of change, however, did not necessarily signify or result from a major departure in American objectives. Secretary of State Dean Rusk, arguing before the Senate Foreign Relations Committee in support of the treaty, testified that "three administrations representing both of our great political parties have devoted so much effort in attempting to make progress toward disarmament."[4] Rusk was referring to the fact that the test ban initiative had originated in the Eisenhower administration, where the president, according to Herbert York, a former member of the General Advisory Committee of the Arms Control and Disarmament Agency, "just like President Kennedy, was very much concerned about where the world was heading and that something ought to be done."[5] Kennedy, in pressing for an arms control agreement, was essentially reviving a policy that had first attracted serious governmental attention in the administration of his Republican predecessor and subsequently foundered at the negotiating table.

The Kennedy administration's policy toward the Soviet Union in 1963 also contained strong residual elements of the Cold War rigidity that had characterized previous administrations and the earlier years of his presidency. At the end of June 1963 in West Berlin Kennedy employed harsh rhetoric in depicting the ideological gulf between East and West. Coming only two weeks after his conciliatory address at American University, it reiterated themes that were strikingly at variance with the new thaw in superpower relations. Moreover, Kennedy refused to consider seriously negotiations with Premier Nikita Khrushchev over a nonaggression pact and coupled his efforts for the limited test ban with promises to accelerate the underground nuclear testing program. Perhaps most illustrative of Kennedy's continued hard-line approach to the Soviet Union and communism was his sustained effort to seek a military solution to the Viet Nam imbroglio.

Addressing himself to the apparent contradictions between the administration's hostile and conciliatory gestures, Richard Walton, one of the most eminent revisionist critics of Kennedy's foreign policy, contended that "in language and deed the President moved toward friendlier relations with Russia, but in neither language nor deed was he consistent."[6] Walton, however, failed to note both the deliberate nature of Kennedy's ambivalence and the conformity of these inconsistencies with the behavior of previous postwar administrations. Arthur M. Schlesinger, Jr., noted in his outstanding memoir of the Kennedy administration, *A Thousand Days*, that the president, despite congressional obtuseness on the matter, consistently linked the extraction of Soviet concessions on arms control to the maintenance of a strong and vigilant defense establishment.[7] More significantly, the Kennedy policy of "talon and olive branch," as the president called it, was broadly consistent with the policies that had developed in the aftermath of World War II. It was a policy dictated by the core objectives of the nation, the encumbrances of domestic politics, and the limitations imposed by the international system. As Theodore Sorensen, one of Kennedy's closest aides, acknowledged, even had the president been elected by an overwhelming majority, "his foreign policy objectives, as distinguished from his methods, would not, I believe, have differed radically from those of his Republican predecessor."[8]

Considering that Kennedy essentially elaborated on a test ban policy that had originated in the Eisenhower administration and that his "peaceful" overtures to the Soviet Union were offered in conjunction with hard-line policies, why did tensions appear to ease in 1963? One obvious and in fact quite convincing explanation lies in the changes that occurred in Soviet policy that year. Buffeted on the one hand by his increasingly bitter dispute with the People's Republic of China and on the other hand by declines in the Soviet economy, Khrushchev accepted the offer of a limited ban on July 2, thereby acquiescing in a proposal that the Soviets had resolutely rejected at Geneva. Later that year, it was the Soviets who initiated contacts with American grain merchants and government officials to engineer a deal for the sale of American wheat to the Soviet Union.

Changes in Soviet policy do not, however, explain in themselves the shift in relations that occurred in 1963. The Soviets had offered to relax tensions earlier, both during the Eisenhower administration and during the early days of the Kennedy administration, but both administrations were reluctant to enter into serious agreements as long as the Soviets continued to vitiate their accommodationist policies with provocations in areas such as Berlin, what was then called the Congo, and Southeast Asia.[9] In 1963, however, the appearance of Soviet willingness to enter into serious negotiations touched off within the Kennedy administration a ripple effect in numerous areas covering a variety of outstanding issues. Clearly, the momentum toward accommodation, limited as it was, was a derivative of a congruence between internal as well as external factors.

What moved the administration to capitalize on opportunities presented by the Soviet leadership in 1963? One conventional and quite plausible explanation lies in Kennedy's personal reaction to the near cataclysm of October 1962. According to this argument, the president was so shaken by the Cuban missile crisis that he was doubly determined to reach a nuclear arms accord with the Soviet Union. In terms of motivation, the events of October clearly had a sobering effect on Chairman Khrushchev. In a speech delivered to an East German audience in January 1963 the Soviet premier, reflecting on the lesson of the Cuban crisis, commented that the revolutionary movement of the working class could not be detached from "the struggle for peace . . . and the prevention of thermonuclear war." Later that year, *Saturday Review* editor Norman Cousins, acting as an intermediary between Kennedy and Khrushchev, was struck by the anxious reaction of the Soviet leader to the missile crisis.[10] It is much more difficult, however, to gauge the effect of the crisis on Kennedy himself. In his correspondence with the Soviet premier, the president alluded to the importance of the crisis in demonstrating the need for some early agreement on a test ban. Nevertheless, whether the crisis had significant impact in changing American policy is questionable. For one thing, Kennedy had demonstrated sufficient concern and interest in arms control even before the missile crisis. Second, despite some initial confusion as to the direction of American policy regarding a comprehensive ban, the missile crisis did not lead to any qualitative relaxation in the American position on the inspection issue. This was in contradistinction to Khrushchev's post-crisis offer to allow three inspections, an offer that the Soviets had been unwilling to concede since the early days of test ban negotiations.[11]

It is possible to argue that among significant elements of the executive branch was a feeling that grew in 1963 that the Sino-Soviet rift was indeed authentic and that American policy should seek to drive a wedge between the Communist rivals. This perception confirmed the assumption that the Soviets were prepared to act out of national interest rather than ideology, a theory that was gaining ground among academic Kremlinologists. This argument has substantial merit, and it will be considered in greater detail later in this book. At the same time, three points must be considered. First, from the inception of his presidency, Kennedy gave greater credence to national than to ideological determinants in explaining Soviet nuclear policy. It is, therefore, highly unlikely that in 1963 he began to see a move away from ideology as a significant explanation for Soviet policy. Second, both publicly and privately, the president tended to be cautious about the permanence of the Sino-Soviet dispute. Third, Kennedy, particularly in his response to the Viet Nam situation, continued to treat the Communist movement as monolithic rather than as polycentric. In so doing, he carried on the policy of active military containment of Soviet influence that began with Korea, receded during the Eisenhower years of massive retaliation, and revived with the strategy of "flexible response."

The détente of 1963 occurred, not because the Kennedy administration developed drastically new objectives in its foreign policy stance toward the Soviet Union, but because of three related factors. First, whereas Eisenhower was personally committed to relaxing the arms race and seeking some mutual areas of agreement between the superpowers, he, unlike Kennedy, did not appear to have a strategic concept that recognized the coexistence of continued political conflict on the one hand and limited military collaboration to avert or restrain nuclear war on the other. Eisenhower's personal interpretation of his cost-cutting "New Look" strategy, with its emphasis on nuclear weapons, was perhaps motivated by a desire to "reduce the pressures for competitive escalation,"[12] and his commitments to disarmament measures and summitry were obviously strong. Nevertheless, the president's inability or disinclination to develop a military strategy that contained the modalities for arms control coupled with Secretary of State John Foster Dulles's belief that arms control measures were of little value in the absence of political accommodation constrained his attempts to achieve accord. Kennedy, on the other hand, inherited Eisenhower's stymied test ban policy but fit it into a strategic and political design that was considerably more integrated as an arms control policy. He was therefore able to view arms control agreements with the Soviets in terms of an objective, reciprocal interest in arrangements for stabilizing the "balance of terror."

Second, Eisenhower's personal commitment to a relaxation of tensions with the Soviet Union was impeded by his constricted view of the presidency. Eisenhower's style of operation within the executive branch allowed the bureaucracy considerable opportunity to obstruct or dilute presidential preferences. Consequently, major bureaucratic players such as Dulles, Lewis Strauss, and John McCone were able, sometimes together and occasionally individually, to frustrate the president's initiatives. Kennedy, on the other hand, with a greater willingness either to circumvent bureaucratic constraints or to lobby vigorously for his own position, was much better able to translate his personal preferences into administration-wide policies.

Third, both Eisenhower and Kennedy operated within the context of a domestic environment that was strongly anti-Soviet in orientation. Kennedy, however, was much more inclined to employ the resources of his office to challenge the political system. Under Kennedy, the principal opposition to a test ban did not lie in the executive branch—except for, and to varying degrees, the Joint Chiefs of Staff—but rather in Congress, where a coalition of Southern and defense-oriented Democrats along with conservative Republicans had been using the Joint Committee on Atomic Energy and the Preparedness Investigating Subcommittee to attack the administration's apparent willingness to negotiate a comprehensive pact prohibiting underground nuclear testing. In 1963 the attacks against the administration's test ban policy were accompanied by Republican efforts to generate political capital out of the Cuban imbroglio and continued congressional hostility to the expansion of trade relations with the Soviet Union. Kennedy dealt with this opposition, in part, by tailoring his decisions to accommodate the public mood and by convincing Congress that his policies did not violate the national consensus. Moreover, he used his office to undertake independent foreign policy actions, circumvent his opposition, and mobilize public support.

The détente of 1963, therefore, reflected strategic policy decisions and a political calculation of the limits to which the domestic political system could be tested. The major policy decision was made in 1962, when the president authorized negotiation of both a comprehensive pact and a partial treaty.

Nevertheless, political calculations were never very far from the heart of test ban policy itself. In 1963, with the Soviets relaying a willingness to negotiate a partial treaty, Kennedy determined that he would stake the prestige of his office on winning endorsement for a limited détente. In doing so, he pressed the political system to accept the existence of policy ambivalences as legitimate expressions of the national interest.

NOTES

1. *Newsweek*, 5 August 1963.
2. *Newsweek*, 7 October 1963, p. 29.
3. See the testimony of General Maxwell D. Taylor, chairman, U.S. Joint Chiefs of Staff, U.S., Congress, Senate, Committee on Foreign Relations, *Hearings: Nuclear Test Ban Treaty*, 88th Cong., 1st sess., 1963, pp. 275-76.
4. *Hearings: Nuclear Test Ban Treaty*, p. 12.
5. Herbert York, recorded interview by Steven Rivkin, June 16, 1964, page 18. John F. Kennedy Library Oral History Program.
6. Richard J. Walton, *Cold War and Revolution* (New York: Viking Press, 1972), p. 143.
7. Arthur M. Schlesinger, Jr., *A Thousand Days* (Boston: Houghton Mifflin, 1965; Fawcett, 1967), p. 469.
8. Theodore C. Sorensen, *Kennedy* (New York: Harper and Row, 1965), p. 510.
9. For an account of missed opportunities during the Eisenhower administration, see Emmet John Hughes, *The Ordeal of Power* (New York: Atheneum, 1963; Dial, 1964), pp. 87-107. See also Bruce Miroff, *Pragmatic Illusions: The Presidential Politics of John F. Kennedy* (New York: McKay, 1976), pp. 46-47.
10. U.S., Arms Control and Disarmament Agency, *Documents on Disarmament, 1963*, p. 12. See also Norman Cousins, *The Improbable Triumvirate* (New York: Norton, 1972), p. 45.
11. This offer was contained in a letter dated December 19, 1962, from Khrushchev to Kennedy, *Documents on Disarmament, 1962*, 2 vols., 2: 1239-42.
12. Paul Y. Hammond, *Cold War and Detente* (New York: Harcourt, Brace, Jovanovich, 1975), p. 145.

3.
JOHN F. KENNEDY, ARMS CONTROL, AND THE SOVIET UNION

Continuity in American foreign policy after World War II derives in large part from the attempts of successive administrations to seek a balance between the goals of anticommunism and avoidance of nuclear war. To be sure, the threat of a serious nuclear exchange between the superpowers did not materialize until the early years of the Eisenhower administration. Nevertheless, President Truman's anti-Communist policies were clearly tempered by his administration's reluctance to engage the Soviet Union in a general war. While anticommunism was defined in global terms, Truman was quite selective about those areas in which the United States would commit its economic and military resources against communism. In part, this caution reflected his assessment that the domestic political system would not support the cost of a massive military and economic commitment. At the same time, the relatively limited nuclear capabilities of the country forced the administration into the realization that a nuclear monopoly alone could not insure complete victory over the Soviet Union.[1]

With the advent of a Soviet nuclear capability, the Truman administration began to reassess its strategic posture. Under the guidelines of NSC-68 and with the impetus of the Korean War, the country shifted into a high-gear rearmament program, involving both a buildup in conventional forces and a decision to develop a hydrogen bomb. NSC-68 represented the first instance during the Cold War in which an administration systematically explored the changing character of force requirements in an era of nuclear war.

The Eisenhower administration assumed power promising to

confront communism vigorously while simultaneously reducing
the country's enormous defense burden. Under a policy vari-
ously referred to as the "New Look" or "Massive Retaliation,"
the administration developed a defense posture relying heavily
on tactical and strategic nuclear weapons. Underlying this
strategy was the assumption that nuclear forces alone could
deter the Soviets from any threat to America's global interests.
In order to reconcile this deterrence strategy with the goal of
nuclear war avoidance, the administration developed a situa-
tional policy known as "brinkmanship." According to Jerome
Kahan, brinkmanship involved the issuance of explicit threats
to employ nuclear weapons in specific instances against strategic
targets.[2] The credibility of the deterrent was supposedly enhanced by the administration's self-imposed inability to conduct limited war.

The Eisenhower administration in operation was far more
restrained than it otherwise threatened to be. One reason for
this restraint was the growing realization in Washington that
American nuclear forces could not destroy Soviet capabilities
enough to preclude a damaging retaliatory strike. This perception grew during the Eisenhower years, as the Soviets increased
their bomber force and surged ahead of the United States in
the development and accumulation of middle-range and long-
range intercontinental ballistic missiles. As a consequence,
marginal threats to American interests involving direct or indirect Soviet provocations led to the employment of non-
nuclear forces, as it did in Lebanon, or to inaction, as in the
cases of Indochina and Hungary. Lebanon, however, was
an exception, and even Eisenhower acknowledged that had
American forces met strong resistance, the intervention would
have seriously strained America's nonnuclear capabilities.[3]

The Eisenhower administration through most of its tenure
operated on two levels: one declaratory, the other actual.[4]
By claiming its readiness to engage in a nuclear strike to defeat
any Soviet threat to American interests, the administration was
obviously signaling its willingness to employ the most drastic
of weapons to contain or even roll back Soviet gains. At the
level of reality, however, Eisenhower was clearly unwilling to
risk nuclear war to arrest Soviet encroachments that did not
directly jeopardize the security of the United States. To critics
of Eisenhower's strategy, the articulated readiness to employ
nuclear weapons, despite its belligerent tone, undermined the
policy of anticommunism. Because the nuclear threat was un-

clear and, more seriously, of questionable credibility, the policy of massive retaliation invited the Soviets to make piecemeal gains on the West.

Eisenhower's constraint of American nuclear forces did not, however, signify his acceptance of an arms control policy. Arms control rests on the proposition that even in the absence of a political solution to the Cold War, each side can design mutually accommodative strategies to avert or limit the possibilities of full-scale nuclear conflict. During most of the Eisenhower administration, arms control policy was inhibited by Secretary Dulles's refusal to seek mutually beneficial spheres of military understanding as long as major political questions remained unsettled. Only with his death and subsequent replacement by Christian Herter did the administration begin to move more seriously toward a test ban treaty.

More importantly, the doctrine of massive retaliation was antithetical to arms control. To be sure, Dulles and Eisenhower did not see the New Look from the same perspective. To Dulles, constrained by the president's stringent fiscal demands, the doctrine represented a supposedly clear pronouncement of American intent to employ its maximum powers to combat communism. To Eisenhower, influenced greatly by Secretary of the Treasury George Humphrey, the New Look was designed to provide the United States with maximum security at the least possible cost. More subtly, the New Look, with its strict control of military spending, may have represented Eisenhower's way of inducing the Soviets to curb the arms race. To Eisenhower, the problem of nuclear war was essentially an arms race problem.

Placing limits on the number of nuclear weapons did not, however, translate into a policy of arms control as long as the administration—and more specifically Dulles—was unrestrained in its threats to use those weapons. Eisenhower opted—until domestic "missile gap" pressures forced him to expand American nuclear forces—for a force posture of sufficiency; he was not willing to employ a "maximum deterrence" strategy, which many in the air force were pressing upon him. Instead, he placed limits on the number of nuclear weapons while simultaneously declaring through Dulles that nuclear warfare formed the core of the American defense posture. Thus, whatever restraint he might have induced in the Soviet position by limiting nuclear forces was undercut by a policy that recognized, at least in theory, few limits to the use of those weapons.

In essence, the policy of massive retaliation militated against the evolution of a Soviet-American understanding on stabilizing the arms race. Soviet leaders viewed the strategy as provocative and threatening to their security. They responded, by and large, with truculent rhetoric, exaggerated boasts, and more importantly by accelerating the pace of their missile development program. Brinkmanship might have deterred the Soviets and their Chinese allies in certain situations, but it also generated a negative action-reaction cycle that made arms stabilization increasingly problematical.[5]

The strategic doctrine of the Kennedy administration was in large part a reaction to the perceived deficiencies of the Eisenhower "New Look" and the changing character and magnitude of Soviet nuclear power. Kennedy was greatly influenced by the strategic studies of the Rand Corporation, academic works by political scientists such as William Kaufmann and Henry Kissinger, and the public criticisms of General Maxwell D. Taylor arguing for the adoption of a flexible options military strategy as a credible alternative to massive retaliation.[6] Kennedy made these criticisms into a central focus of his campaign for the presidency.

Moreover, Kennedy used the highly volatile "missile gap" issue to score points against his Republican opponent, Vice-President Richard M. Nixon. Because of the accelerated pace of Soviet missile development and the increasingly bellicose boasts of Soviet Premier Nikita S. Khrushchev regarding the superiority of his country's nuclear capabilities, the impression grew in the United States that this country could not insure the destruction of Soviet retaliatory power in a first strike. Worse yet, from the standpoint of the Eisenhower administration, significant sentiment developed around the proposition that the United States would not in the near future be able to sustain the crippling effects of a surprise attack. This argument was given great credibility by the report of the blue-ribbon Gaither committee, warning, on the heels of the traumatic Sputnik launching, that American reliance on the survivability of the strategic air command (SAC) bomber force was becoming increasingly tenuous.

To be sure, by the last two years of his second term Eisenhower was arriving at similar conclusions. For one thing, both the president and his secretary of state acknowledged publicly that all-out nuclear war was not the only option in the nuclear age; instead, they contemplated the possibilities of

limited war, both conventional and nuclear.[7] Second, despite
Eisenhower's belief that the Soviets would never strike first[8]
and his attempt to suppress the gloomy analysis of the
Gaither report, the president stepped up efforts to make American nuclear forces less vulnerable to a devastating first strike.
Such measures included the development of an American intercontinental ballistic missile (ICBM) force, the continuous deployment of a portion of the SAC bomber force in the air, and
the completion of an early warning system. Indeed, by the end
of the decade Eisenhower's decision to increase the defense
budget for missile development led to a decisive nuclear advantage over the Soviet Union, which Kennedy learned soon after
his accession to the presidency.

KENNEDY AND THE DEVELOPMENT OF "MULTIPLE OPTIONS"

It was left to Kennedy to develop a systematic strategy that
would balance the goals of anticommunism and nuclear war
avoidance. Kennedy and his secretary of defense Robert
McNamara discovered fairly early in their administration that
the missile gap did not exist. This did not mean, however,
that the country could rely on its nuclear forces alone to deal
with the Soviet threat. With the Soviets continuing to develop
their ICBMs, it was unlikely that in any future first strike the
Americans could completely neutralize the Soviets' second-
strike capability.[9] Consequently in the event of nuclear war,
no matter the initiator and no matter the final outcome in terms
of concrete gains and losses, neither side could claim victory.
As McNamara stated, ". . . there would be such severe damage
to this country that our way of life would change. . . . Therefore, I would say we had not won."[10]

Responding to the realities of Soviet power and to what he
referred to as "our national tradition," Kennedy in his first
major defense message to Congress declared that the United
States would never use its nuclear weapons to "strike the first
blow in any attack."[11] The major focus of strategic policy in
the early months of the Kennedy administration was in protect-
ing American forces and population centers against surprise
Soviet attack. This project involved the hardening and dispersal
of Minuteman land-based missiles and the deployment of a
greater number of Polaris submarines, which had first been
authorized during the Eisenhower administration. It also entailed, with great controversy, the institutionalization of plans

to construct a nationwide shelter program and the development of a command and control system that could withstand
an initial surprise attack.

Kennedy did not believe that Khrushchev would be so reck-
less as to initiate a nuclear exchange and assumed that the continued hardening of American second-strike capabilities would
reinforce the Soviet premier in his reluctance. This view was
buttressed by Khrushchev's speech of January 6, 1961, in which
the chairman rejected the feasibility of general war and even
local conflict as a realistic means to enhance the ultimate
victory of "socialism." Instead, Khrushchev announced his intention to support wars of national liberation and thereby erode
the capitalist world at its periphery. In Kennedy's estimation,
this aspect of the Soviet leader's address posed the greatest challenge to the West.[12] Accordingly, the United States and its allies
would have to develop modalities that could respond effectively
to change in Soviet tactics.

Kennedy's vigorous response to the challenge posed by
Khrushchev's revolutionary exhortations requires some explanation. While it is clear that the speech represented a major exposition on the changing character of conflict in nuclear age, it did
not reveal anything that the Soviets had not already demonstrated in deeds, if not words. By involving themselves so
energetically in Cuba and the Congo, the Soviets had already
shown that they were willing and able to manipulate unstable
political conditions for their own purposes. Why, then, did the
president consider the speech so significant that he read aloud
from it at meetings of the National Security Council? And why
did Secretary McNamara, in a speech delivered to the American
Bar Association in February 1962, refer to it as ". . . one of the
most significant speeches of the past year, and it may prove to
be one of the most important statements made by a world
leader in the decade of the 1960's."[13]

In some respects, the administration publicly employed the
Khrushchev speech to restore confidence in the American deterrent. By rejecting offensive nuclear war as a credible instrument
of his country's foreign policy, the Soviet leader was giving testimony to the awesome destructive power of American nuclear
forces. The administration was interested in conveying this
feeling of confidence to the public in the aftermath of the
missile gap controversy.

More importantly, the Kennedy administration was determined to restore the balance between nuclear war avoidance

and anticommunism, which in Kennedy's estimation the strategy of massive retaliation had undermined. To Kennedy, Eisenhower's policy had created ambiguity in the American definition of anticommunism and hence had induced the Soviets and their allies to threaten American interests through indirect aggressions. Kennedy attempted to restore the balance by defining a wide range of Communist activities as constituting threats to American interests, and he attempted to strengthen the American response by reducing reliance on nuclear forces. Hence, Kennedy's emphasis on nonnuclear means of conflict was designed not only to provide a greater guarantee against the outbreak of nuclear war but also to combat communism in a more effective manner.

Kennedy's was not the first postwar administration to define "wars of liberation" as Communist provocations. The Truman Doctrine had recognized insurgencies in Greece and Turkey as Communist-inspired, and the Eisenhower administration had involved itself in a variety of ways in the internal affairs of Iran, Guatemala, Indonesia, and Lebanon, among other places. Kennedy's, however, was the first administration to make military intervention in these wars a central element of its anti-Communist strategy.

In part, this reflected the president's contention that the major arena of East-West conflict had shifted from Europe to the Third World.[14] Moreover, American involvement in wars of national liberation was designed to serve as a demonstration to the Soviets of the administration's ability to control and escalate its military responses in the face of graduated threats to the national interest. While Kennedy initially placed great emphasis on counterinsurgency warfare as a means to neutralize Communist advances,[15] his policy of escalation in Viet Nam demonstrates that important elements within the administration viewed the conflict as a test case for a strategy of non-nuclear, controlled response. American involvement was designed to show the Soviets and America's Western European allies that the administration possessed the capabilities and resolve to apply force against Soviet-sponsored aggression. As Assistant Secretary of Defense John McNaughton described it in the early 1960s, U.S. involvement in Viet Nam was designed, more than anything else, to preserve America's "reputation as a guarantor."[16]

What was most important about the Khrushchev speech was that it confirmed assumptions about Soviet behavior that tended to justify the multiple options military strategy that

Kennedy's administration was about to introduce. The portrayal of Soviet aims as universal and Soviet means as limited was essential to the establishment of a strategy that would attempt to balance the goals of anticommunism and nuclear war avoidance by tailoring American forces to meet graduated threats to the national interest. As he came into office, Kennedy was as convinced as his predecessors that the long-range goals of the Soviet Union were inimical to America's core interests. He was equally committed to the role of the United States as the principal opponent to communism; as W. Averell Harriman commented, "He had a very clear conception of the Soviet Union and communism . . . he recognized the basic and fundamental difference between us—their desire to communize the world, and our desire to frustrate them in their designs."[17]

At the same time, Kennedy recognized that the dangers of nuclear war placed limits on the exercise of American power. To Kennedy, this recognition linked him to the policies of his predecessors as he explained in a press conference in 1963: "The reason the action wasn't taken was because they [Eisenhower and Truman] felt strongly that if they did take action it would bring on another war."[18] Consequently, a strategy had to be formulated that would contain Soviet expansion without projecting both countries into a cataclysmic general war. Kennedy, who assumed that the Eisenhower strategy was deficient both in arresting the spread of communism and in preventing nuclear catastrophe, attempted to reconstruct the balance by developing modalities that would combat communism and simultaneously avert general war. In this sense, the Khrushchev speech of January 1961 was perfectly suited as a justification for the evolving strategy. By appearing to eschew the employment of nuclear weapons to achieve world domination but by not abandoning the Communist objectives to do so, Khrushchev was lending immediacy to an American strategy that, at least in theory, could adjust more readily to the multifaceted character of Soviet aggression.

FLEXIBLE RESPONSE AND THE WESTERN ALLIANCE

A similar concern guided Kennedy's approach to the Western alliance. With the accession of Charles de Gaulle to power in France and the accelerated French effort to develop a nuclear capability of their own, the president was faced with the specter of political and military fragmentation in an area still considered to be the forward defense against Soviet advance. While the French were also motivated by considerations of national prestige, other European states, particularly the German Federal Republic, were apprehensive about the American willingness to commit nuclear weapons against the Soviet Union in the event of a Soviet attack.

European restiveness about the effectiveness of the American deterrent increased during the Kennedy administration, in large part as a consequence of Kennedy's efforts to employ a multiple options approach in their defense. Under the Eisenhower doctrine of massive retaliation, Europe's shield was provided by the American nuclear force. It was assumed that the Soviets would refrain from hostile action as long as American capabilities were strong and as long as the American commitment to use nuclear weapons in defense of Europe was both clear and credible.[19]

The Kennedy administration, however, believed that the conventional threat was a more plausible deterrent to Soviet aggression. McNamara for one was convinced that Western Europe had escaped from its postwar economic devastation and could now assume a more equitable portion of its own defense burden.[20] Moreover, the administration no longer adhered to the popular European belief that Soviet conventional forces were so great as to render any counterbuildup economically and militarily prohibitive. After an early review of Soviet capabilities, the Defense Department concluded that Soviet conventional strength on the European front was not nearly as formidable as generally estimated. Consequently, according to the administration, alliance strategy had to be geared toward the development of nonnuclear forces, as McNamara reasoned in his famous Ann Arbor address of 1962.[21]

This conflict between the administration and its European allies found each side working at cross-purposes. The Europeans argued that American determination to increase the alliance's conventional strength only demonstrated to the Soviets that the United States was not willing to employ nuclear weapons in case of Soviet attack. By focusing on the development of non-nuclear capabilities, the Americans were debasing their nuclear deterrent. As a result, the Europeans were even more interested in acquiring their own nuclear forces.

The administration, however, felt that the proliferation of independent nuclear forces in the world would ultimately erode

the defensive capabilities of the alliance. Aside from the president's deep personal concern about the dangers of proliferation,
the administration was of the opinion that small nuclear forces
were strategically extraneous and potentially hazardous. This
latter assessment was based on the fear that a small force might
invite preemptive attack and then draw the United States into
a larger war.[22]

Most importantly, the Kennedy administration felt that
European reliance on independent nuclear forces would undermine America's shift to a multiple options strategy and simultaneously threaten the controlled-response nuclear strategy. The
administration assumed that there were gradations of possible
Soviet-bloc attack against Western Europe. If the alliance's conventional forces were too thin, however, their weakness would
invite the kind of Communist encroachment that was certain
of limited conventional success yet calculated to avert a nuclear
response. The administration believed that the development of
small nuclear forces of a nontactical type would place too great
an emphasis on the nuclear deterrent. Hence, the European
members of the alliance would have little incentive to shore up
their conventional defenses. In the face of an ambiguous threat
to a European state the alliance would have two options: nuclear
war or inaction.

The administration's multiple options design for Europe was
thus consistent with its general strategy of containment,
although quite clearly the nuclear option was a much more
likely possibility in the defense of Europe than, for example,
Southeast Asia. By placing greater emphasis on nonnuclear
forces, it could mitigate the military consequences of confrontation and concomitantly strengthen the alliance's ability to deflect the Soviets. Not all European states were of the same opinion. The French proceeded to develop their own nuclear force,
and the British demanded satisfaction of Eisenhower's earlier
offer of Polaris missiles in lieu of the ill-fated Skybolt. The
Americans attempted to ameliorate alliance tensions by placing tactical nuclear weapons in the hands of NATO, as did
Eisenhower, and by proposals such as the multilateral force
(MLF); but they basically adhered to the position that Europe
could best be defended by combining the nuclear deterrent
with a strong conventional capability. In this sense the administration was extending its strategic doctrine to Western Europe—
an area that had since the end of World War II been considered,
from a strategic standpoint, almost as an extension of American territory.

DEFENSE POLICY AT HOME

This is not to say, in terms of American nuclear capabilities, that the new strategic doctrine was necessarily converted into appropriate force levels. The Kennedy-McNamara strategy implied that the nuclear capabilities of the country were essentially deterrent in purpose and hence had to be built up to the point of assured second-strike destruction of the enemy. Graham Allison and Frederic Morris observed, however, that the force levels of the Kennedy administration far exceeded the requirements of the doctrine.[23] In part, this can be explained by continuing American uncertainties about the nuclear capabilities of the Soviet Union. As McNamara wrote in his 1963 posture statement, "One of the major uncertainties is, of course, the size and character of our opponents' strategic forces and defensive systems now, and more importantly, in the future."[24] While it was almost immediately apparent that the missile gap did not exist, the pace of the Soviet development program was uncertain to American policymakers.

Allison and Morris argued that there were other reasons for the gap between the requirements of assured destruction and the actual number of nuclear weapons that were deployed during this period of time.[25] First, Kennedy had promised during his campaign to strengthen strategic forces; to reduce that number in the budget for fiscal year 1962 would have created difficulties in Congress. Second, according to Allison and Morris, the concept of nuclear superiority had become an article of faith enjoying widespread governmental and extragovernmental support in the early years of the Kennedy administration—a fact not lost on McNamara in his subsequent defense of the Test Ban Treaty on Capitol Hill.[26] This consensus produced a momentum for the accumulation of greater numbers of nuclear weapons, even when those numbers exceeded the requirements of the doctrine. The military services, with important allies in the legislature, estimated the required force levels at a much higher number than McNamara and Kennedy. Accordingly, the civilian officials in the administration were compelled to bargain with the military services to achieve a more equitable number that was still beyond the requirements of the strategic doctrine. Third, the defense budgets of the Kennedy years contained costs for some weapons systems that had already been authorized under Eisenhower.

Inconsistencies in the actual force deployment were matched by inconsistencies in doctrine. During the first two years of

the Kennedy administration, the strategic emphasis was on
deterrence, involving in 1961 the hardening and dispersal of
second-strike and command capabilities and in 1962 the development of a counterforce doctrine. But in 1963 McNamara
announced a cities-avoidance strategy, which rested on the
country's ability to strike at military and nonmilitary targets
simultaneously or to strike at military targets and hold cities
captive to a second counterstrike.[27] On the surface, the purpose
of this strategy, combined with a strong counterforce capacity
and civil defense program at home, was to limit the damage to
population centers on both sides in the event deterrence failed.
In actuality, according to its critics, it threatened to undermine deterrence by offering a type of nuclear war that was
more palatable to both sides. While in some respects consistent with the doctrine of graduated response, it also challenged the administration's commitment to nuclear war
avoidance, administration disclaimers to the contrary.

THE LOGIC OF ARMS CONTROL

Doctrinal inconsistencies notwithstanding, Kennedy appears
to have attached high priority to averting nuclear war with the
Soviets. In part, this was supposed to be accomplished by the
creation of military alternatives that made the nuclear option
less supreme. Another method was arms control, which was
clearly at the center of policy-making interest during the
nearly three years of the Kennedy administration. In understanding how arms control fit into Kennedy's military-political
strategy and why he considered it a viable option in the face
of continued Soviet hostility, it would be instructive to divide
the following discussion into two portions, one military and
the other political.

The most visible arms control agreement of the Kennedy
years was the Nuclear Test Ban Treaty. In pressing for its
ratification on Capitol Hill, Secretary of Defense McNamara
offered the administration's definitive strategic rationale for
its acceptance and in so doing, assessed the state of U.S.-U.S.S.R.
weapons development in 1963. Clearly, the principal area of
concern for domestic critics of the treaty was the constraint it
would impose on the development of high-yield weapons,
which required atmospheric detonations for effective testing.
The administration conceded that the Soviets enjoyed a
definite superiority in this area. Nevertheless, in explaining the

treaty to the Senate, McNamara argued that the administration
saw greater value in the development of low-yield weapons
and could easily tolerate a Soviet advantage in high-yield
weaponry.[28]

According to McNamara, while high-yield weapons dropped
from high altitudes caused tremendous thermal fires over
large cities, a larger number of smaller weapons could produce
the same impact and have a better chance of saturating enemy
defenses. In addition, while high-yielding weapons could destroy hard-shell command posts, even they could not penetrate
extremely deep installations. In this regard, they were no more
effective than numerous low-yield weapons.

While arguing that the United States, even under the terms
of the Test Ban Treaty, could most probably develop high-
yield weapons of a fifty-to-sixty megaton range for B-52 delivery, McNamara essentially reasoned that the strategic calculations of the Kennedy administration precluded such a costly
and perhaps useless enterprise. With regard to the other major
area of concern, ABM development, McNamara contended that
extrapolation from available data along with continued underground testing could sufficiently enhance warhead technology
and resistance to blackout effects, two areas that depended on
nuclear testing.[29] With regard to countering Soviet ABM technology, McNamara admitted that greater knowledge of warhead invulnerability upon reentry could be achieved by atmospheric testing. Nevertheless, according to the secretary of
defense, the size of the American nuclear force along with
testing and extrapolative capabilities under the terms of the
treaty could effectively neutralize a Soviet ABM system at its
existing stage of development.[30]

The administration's commitment to arms control was not
confined to the search for a workable test ban agreement alone.
Instead, arms control pervaded the entire military doctrine of
the Kennedy administration. In this respect, it is evident that
Kennedy's nuclear and conventional strategy was heavily influenced by the Harvard-MIT Arms Control Seminar conducted
in 1960-61. Theories and recommendations of the most influential members of the seminar were incisively summarized in
Strategy and Arms Control, written by Thomas C. Schelling
and Morton H. Halperin.[31] The essential argument of the
monograph is that political differences notwithstanding, the
superpowers shared a common interest in managing the arms
race in order to avoid nuclear war, limit one should it occur,

and generally moderate the threat perception inherent in the reciprocal fear of surprise attack. Security against surprise attack through nuclear deterrence was given a surprising twist. Stability of mutual deterrence was seen as being more certain at higher rather than lower levels of armaments. The result was a clear rejection of disarmament as a superior road to peace. Sound defense policies on both sides would lead to the procurement of systems that would reduce the benefits of a surprise attack. In short, a central aspect of arms control thinking in Cambridge was military collaboration with the Soviet Union in the acquisition of new nuclear weapons systems, whether through unilateral decisions that are reciprocated or through negotiated agreements limiting both sides in their choice and testing of weapons.

The impact of this theory on the arms control thinking of the Kennedy administration is obvious in the words of the assistant secretary of defense, John T. McNaughton, who was the principal administration exponent of the partial test ban initiative. In a speech in 1962 McNaughton observed:

> Another popular assumption is that all arms control measures . . . must be negotiated. This too is wrong. The feature of enhancing simultaneously the security of both sides characterizes a multiplicity of measures running across the spectrum from negotiated disarmament agreements, through reciprocal initiatives and through unilateral acts which involve only rational adjustment by the other side, to purely unilateral measures involving no reciprocation or adjustment by any other country.[32]

McNaughton went on to outline three major areas of arms control strategy:

1. Those designed to prevent wars by "accident."
2. Those designed to prevent wars by miscalculation, . . . to permit deliberate, controlled response, especially in crisis.
3. Those designed to reduce the damage should a war occur—by building firebreaks against escalation of conflict, by pursuing a strategy which is anti-military rather than anti-population, and by ensuring that the power to stop a war is preserved.[33]

The administration saw arms control as part of a sound defense policy designed to reduce the dangerous consequences of

America's protracted conflict with Communist powers. Arms control theories about stable deterrence helped to rationalize an expansion of nuclear forces even to the point of clear superiority. The Soviet leadership, it was reasoned, could assume that the reinforcing cycle of reciprocal fear of surprise attack no longer existed because of American superiority. Moreover, superiority would also reduce the possibility of war through miscalculation or accident. Indeed, from an arms control standpoint, the Hotline Agreement, with its emphasis on avoiding miscalculation and communicating objectives in crisis situations, was perhaps a more significant measure than the Test Ban Treaty. Arms control was, therefore, not a strategy of idealists; instead it was a strategy in the tradition of balance-of-power theories, designed to control or manage conflict.

ARMS CONTROL AND DETENTE—IDEOLOGY VERSUS NATIONAL INTEREST

Aside from the strategic changes that made the test ban a viable agreement from the standpoint of American security, Kennedy tended to view arms control, because it placed a premium on Soviet-American collaboration, as a unique means to ameliorate political tensions. Military collaboration, it was reasoned, might build mutual confidence and hence lessen the explosive potential of reciprocal fears. This link between arms control and détente was a central premise of Kennedy's foreign policy and helps to distinguish it from Eisenhower's initial test ban efforts, where the anticipated political payoff—in terms of better Soviet-American relations—was much less clearly understood.

To be sure, Kennedy did see propagandistic value in a declaratory policy in favor of disarmament, despite his practical objections to disarmament. Schlesinger recalled that in preparing the American presentation to the 1961 meeting of the General Assembly, United Nations Ambassador Adlai Stevenson argued for the inclusion of a disarmament proposal. The president responded that Congress's cool reception to the proposed Arms Control and Disarmament Agency demonstrated that disarmament was not a popular issue in the United States. Nevertheless, Kennedy welcomed Stevenson's idea as a means by which the United States could "make time against the Soviet Union."[34] Sorensen cited a similar case involving the president's issuance of guidelines to the administration's arms control task force in 1962. Kennedy asked the negotiators to meet broad

Soviet initiatives with "proposals that were not so complex and cautious as to lack all force and appeal."[35]

Despite these initial motives, Kennedy did not view arms control progress as significantly unrelated to the conduct of relations in other sensitive political areas. Former Democratic Senate Majority Leader Mike Mansfield remembered that Kennedy ". . . thought it [Test Ban Treaty] might increase the thaw, might open paths which had hitherto remained closed, and might mark a beginning in a better relationship between the Soviets and ourselves."[36]

To Kennedy and his advisers, arms control was the one issue that had become almost a symbol of Soviet-American cooperation and competition in the Cold War era. According to this line of thought, relations in general could be judged by the failure or success of both sides to negotiate arms control agreements. This point was underscored by Arms Control and Disarmament Agency (ACDA) member Franklin Long in a letter to Kennedy dated July 12, 1963:

> The test ban negotiations have come to represent almost an institutional barrier to improved relations between the two countries, and failure of the two countries to resolve this issue has symbolized their inability to reach agreement on the central problems of the Cold War.[37]

To be sure, Kennedy continued to view Soviet foreign policy as essentially expansionistic[38] and thus realized that arms control did not carry with it an end to Cold War hostility. Instead, détente, according to the president's rather modest interpretation, involved a widening of cooperative areas and a defusion of flashpoints, leaving the central antagonism intact. In defending his policy to the American people, Kennedy quite pointedly explained to a public schooled in the Manichaeism of the Dulles era that ambivalences were legitimate expressions of the national interest. On July 26, 1963, in a radio and television address in support of the Nuclear Test Ban Treaty, Kennedy commented, "It [the Nuclear Test Ban Treaty] will not resolve all conflicts, or cause the Communists to forego their ambitions, or eliminate the danger of war."[39] And in a fuller statement on the ambivalences of détente, Kennedy told an audience at the University of Maine:

> . . . there is nothing inconsistent with signing an atmospheric nuclear test ban, on the one hand, and testing underground

on the other; about being willing to sell the Soviets our
surplus wheat while refusing to sell strategic items; or
about exploring the possibilities of disarmament while
maintaining a stockpile of arms.[40]

Kennedy was essentially stating what had already become
fundamental to American foreign policy—that the American
approach to the Soviet Union involved an amalgam of accommodative and confrontational policies. In Kennedy's case, however, the evolution of a balanced strategy was more deliberate
and theoretically based than it had been under Truman and
Eisenhower. For Kennedy was, above all, a pragmatist who
viewed the Cold War, particularly at the nuclear level, as a conflict of interests rather than of ideologies.

The notion that the Soviet Union, in the aftermath of the
Cuban missile crisis, was demonstrating a distinct interest in
accommodation and thus vitiating its ideological antagonism
to the West was one to which many in and outside the administration attached great credence. The most comprehensive
assessment of this kind was provided by a politically influential Kremlinologist, Marshall D. Shulman of Tufts University's Fletcher School of Law and Diplomacy, in an exposition
before the Senate Foreign Relations Committee.[41] Shulman
argued that the Soviet leadership in 1963 was preoccupied with
economic and political problems on the domestic front, fissures
within the Soviet bloc, and increasing restiveness in the world
Communist movement. For these reasons, the Soviets were
compelled to moderate their conflict with the United States.
Perhaps more important in the long run, according to Shulman,
was the fact that:

> The most striking characteristic of recent Soviet foreign
> policy has been the way in which policies undertaken for
> short-term, expediential purposes have tended to elongate
> in time, and become embedded in doctrine and political
> strategy. The shift to a "peaceful coexistence" emphasis,
> originally a tactical alternation, has been evolving and
> deepening into a policy directed to power-bloc politics
> rather than toward social revolution.[42]

Shulman suggested that the shift to a more "benign" policy
on the part of the Soviet Union would most likely depend on
the extent to which American foreign policy responded in kind.

In other words, Shulman was urging American policymakers to cease viewing the Soviets as creatures of ideology exclusively and begin exploring the nuances in Soviet behavior for evidence of pragmatic self-interest. By developing policies that increased the Soviet stake in peace and stability, American decision makers could, in fact, elevate the temporary Soviet interest into a key aspect of dogma.

Kennedy, too, believed that the Soviet national interest could lead to a relaxation of tensions with the United States, but he did not subscribe to a "benign" view of Soviet policy. While the president saw arms control as an area of potential accommodation, he recognized that the Soviets would continue to challenge American interests through wars of national libera- tion and other forms of provocation. For these reasons, he pursued a test ban without pressing the Soviets vigorously for collateral political agreements on, for example, Europe and Southeast Asia. Neither did he accept the recommendation of adviser W. W. Rostow to make a test ban contingent on gain- ing political concessions from the Soviets on Cuba, Laos, and Viet Nam.[43] Kennedy believed that there could be some superpower reciprocation in the nuclear field. He also felt that nuclear accommodation might attenuate Soviet ambitions in other areas, but only because arms control signified Soviet acceptance of American capabilities to frustrate their objec- tives through limited and controlled military responses. At the same time, he persisted in recognizing Soviet policy as inher- ently opportunistic and continued to treat wars of national liberation as extensions of the Soviet national interest.

Whereas Shulman saw Cuba as a watershed in Soviet-Ameri- can relations, the crisis, rather than changing Kennedy's approach to the Kremlin, confirmed what the president already knew—that the Soviets were not willing to risk their own destruc- tion for some transitory political or strategic gain. To be sure, the crisis impressed on Kennedy the Soviet desire to avoid nuclear holocaust. On December 17, 1962, the president told a nationwide audience, "I do think his [Khrushchev's] speech shows he realizes how dangerous a world we live in."[44] And in a magazine interview published in August 1963, Kennedy stated, "I am sure that the event had a sobering effect on Mr. Khrushchev."[45] Moreover, it probably made it more imperative for Kennedy, from a psychological standpoint, to seek a solu- tion to the test ban imbroglio. Schlesinger was clearly impressed by the effects of Cuba on the president: "As for Kennedy, his feelings underwent a qualitative change after Cuba; a world in which nations threatened each other with nuclear weapons seemed to him not just as irrational but an intolerable and impossible world."[46]

It would be a mistake, however, to see the Cuban crisis as giving the president a new perspective on Soviet policy that de-emphasized the militant, ideological portrait that had dominated American thinking throughout the Cold War, for Kennedy—at least as a public man—never really subscribed to the point of view that ideology was the principal source of Soviet foreign policy. The Cuban missile crisis, the agreement of the Soviets to negotiate a partial test ban treaty, and the Soviet initiative to buy wheat from American grain merchants did not, therefore, signify to Kennedy the sudden ascendancy of *realpolitik* tendencies in the Kremlin. Instead, they confirmed what Kennedy believed all along—that the Soviets operated according to national interest rather than ideological motives, at least at the level of nuclear politics. In explaining this phenomenon to the American people, Kennedy rejected the notion that the intrusion of ideology onto the international scene in the twentieth century had significantly rigidified the conduct of international relations. Instead, he seemed to assert something equivalent to a nineteenth-century "balance-of-power" concept of alliance building and disintegration with its constant fluidity in international friendships and enmities. In his American University address, the president declared, "And history teaches us that enmities between nations as between individuals do not last forever. However fixed our likes and dislikes may seem the tide of time and events will often bring surprising shifts in the relations."[47] And on September 26, 1963, Kennedy stated his concept of national interest:

> . . . we must recognize that every nation determines its policies in terms of its own interests. . . . National interest is more powerful than ideology, and the recent developments within the Communist empire show this very clearly. Friendship, as Palmerston said, may rise and wane, but interests endure.[48]

These comments represented clear references to what was perceived by many in 1963 as a major split in the Communist world, with the Soviet Union and the People's Republic of China at odds over a variety of issues including the crucial doc-

trine of "peaceful coexistence." The administration first accorded serious attention to this dispute in 1961, under the
auspices of the State Department's Bureau of Intelligence and
Research, and in January 1962 the upper levels of the department began to consider it a significant international development.[49] In November 1962 Roger Hilsman of the Bureau of
Intelligence and Research delivered a major speech on the
Sino-Soviet dispute and attacked the impression that it was
a hoax.

By the time the Senate examined the Nuclear Test Ban Treaty,
even the Joint Chiefs, who were probably most distrustful
within the administration of Soviet motives, acknowledged that
the Sino-Soviet dispute was authentic.[50] In a research memorandum dated June 14, 1963, from Thomas Hughes of the
Bureau of Intelligence and Research (INR) to Secretary of
State Rusk, the intelligence expert suggested that Khrushchev
himself most probably calculated that American policymakers
saw the Soviet Union as being at a major turning point in its
foreign policy."[51]

Kennedy himself recognized the seriousness of the conflict.
During his visit to West Berlin in June 1963, the president was
given a detailed rundown on the internecine Communist dispute by Ambassador Foy Kohler.[52] And in numerous public
speeches and press conferences he employed the theme of
Sino-Soviet discord to score debating points against communism
and to reaffirm the strength of the West in the face of a fragmented enemy. For example, in his 1963 State of the Union
address, the president commented, ". . . it was only a few years
ago . . . that communism sought to convey the image of a
unified, confident and expanding empire. . . . But few people
would hold to that picture today."[53] In a magazine article
published the following day, Kennedy was even more emphatic
in pointing to the disintegration of the Communist world:
"Within the Communist world itself, monolithic unity has begun to give way to the forces of diversity that are bursting the
bonds of both organization and ideology—heated arguments
have become the rule instead of the exception."[54]

Nevertheless, when called upon to assess the long-range policy
implications of the Sino-Soviet dispute, the president was considerably more circumspect. In a July 17, 1963, press conference, following the apparent collapse of Soviet-Chinese
reconciliation efforts, Kennedy reflected on the permanence

of the dispute, "Quite obviously there are strong indications of pressure there, but I would not make any final statements because history has shown that they are frequently reversed."[55] In fact, according to Sorensen, the president ". . . derived little comfort from the Soviet-Chinese dispute, and thought, on the contrary, that it might increase the dangers of desperation in Moscow or irresponsibility in Peking,"[56] even though he recognized that the ". . . new fluidity in the post-Cuba Communist camp . . . presented opportunities which seventeen years of cold war rigidities had never made possible before."[57]

To Kennedy, the Sino-Soviet rift, with all its dangers and possibilities, was less a revelation than a confirmation of his belief that national interest, not ideology, was the principal engine of Soviet foreign policy. According to Schlesinger, Kennedy, "unlike the ideological interpreters of the Cold War . . . was not surprised by the split between Russia and China."[58] The selection of a military strategy with multiple options, the pursuit of functional agreements of a technical nature, and most importantly the diplomatic effort to achieve a nuclear test ban accord all rested on the assumption that the Soviets could be expected to interpret their ideology to conform to immediate and long-range power interests. The growing corrosion in the Soviet-Chinese relationship, therefore, did not give rise to the need for a new diplomatic effort so much as it confirmed the wisdom of existing policies. In retrospect, the greatest significance of the split was in justifying to recalcitrant segments of the executive branch the wisdom of a policy of limited accommodation. General Curtis LeMay, in testifying before the Senate in 1963, acknowledged that his qualified approval of the treaty was in large part a consequence of assiduous lobbying efforts by Harriman and Rusk who argued that the treaty would only further worsen Sino-Soviet relations.[59]

Within the administration, Kennedy was clearly the foremost exponent of the view that the wellsprings of Soviet behavior were to be found in national interest rather than ideology. This point is evidenced not only by his public speeches but by the testimony of numerous advisers and political allies. Schlesinger wrote, for example, that, "He [Kennedy] never took ideology very seriously, certainly not as a means of interpreting history . . . he tended to give greater weight in thinking about world affairs to national rather than to ideological motives."[60]

To his friends, this was a serious weakness in his understanding of Soviet behavior. According to Charles ("Chip") Bohlen, Kennedy

> didn't quite understand it [the ideological aspects of the Cold War] because I don't believe—I never had the impression—that President Kennedy had seriously read Marx or Lenin, or any of the Soviet theoretical writers very much . . . any of the subtleties of its application by the Russians, I felt was somewhat of a closed book to him.[61]

British Prime Minister Harold Macmillan, a Kennedy admirer, was equally impressed by the president's undue minimization of the ideological aspects of the Soviet-American conflict:

> There is a marked difference between President Kennedy "in action" on a specific problem . . . and his attitude to larger issues (the nuclear war, the struggle between East and West, Capitalism and Communism, etc). In the first, he is an extraordinarily quick and effective operator— a born "politician" . . . On the wider issues, he seems rather lost. . . .[62]

This assessment was corroborated by U. Alexis Johnson, under Kennedy the undersecretary for political affairs in the Department of State:

> [Kennedy] was not what I would call a philosophical or a subjective turn of mind . . . and if he had a weakness I would say that it was a tendency to decide in the light of the immediate circumstances at the time without trying to look far ahead.[63]

Kennedy's tendency to "discount, at times perhaps unduly the role of dogma in Soviet policy,"[64] was illustrated most pointedly in his 1961 summit meeting with Khrushchev in Vienna. In that meeting, the president attempted to engage the Soviet premier in an ideological colloquy, but the inexperienced Kennedy was clearly outmatched by his practiced opponent. According to Schlesinger, Kennedy "might have done better by eschewing ideological discussion."[65] Instead, the president tried to induce Khrushchev to accept Kennedy's nonideological interpretation of Soviet behavior. Llewellyn

Thompson, a Kennedy confidant and recognized expert on Soviet affairs, was especially pained by Kennedy's approach:

> I think in retrospect, I'm sorry in a way that the discussion got off on ideological grounds . . . which is something I don't think the President quite appreciated the fact that a Communist like Mr. Khrushchev could not yield even if he wanted to. I mean he couldn't formally deny his own ideology.[66]

Kennedy's view of national interest as a determining factor in Soviet foreign policy implied not that the ideology was inoperative, but that it would take a back seat to national interest when the two came into conflict. Whereas Dulles, with his rigid, ideological interpretation of the Cold War, was reluctant to engage the Soviets in any agreement, Kennedy and others in his administration believed that the Soviets could reciprocate positively as long as reciprocation enhanced their national interest. Accordingly, the Soviets could initial and even observe arms control agreements but continue to support wars of national liberation, so long as such support did not threaten the national interest.

In some respects, Kennedy's arms control policy can be seen as a diplomatic weapon in the Cold War. On one level, the president sponsored a plan for the general and complete disarmament which was viewed as a propaganda instrument designed to meet similar, sweeping Soviet disarmament proposals at the United Nations. Given the "general disarmament" component of Sino-Soviet polemics, the administration thereby hoped to further the public debate within the Communist bloc. More importantly, by embracing the arms control strategy of military collaboration, the Soviets were induced to take a position on the hotline and nuclear testing diametrically opposed to China's.

Most importantly, the Kennedy arms control policy represented an attempt by its architects to strengthen the anti-Communist component in American military strategy. Eisenhower had effectively avoided nuclear war, but according to his critics, he did so too precariously and at the expense of anticommunism. Under Kennedy, arms control was designed to stabilize the nuclear relationship between the superpowers and in so doing free the United States to confront the Soviets in a more flexible manner. In order to insure the necessary stability for a more effective anti-Communist strategy, the administration had to cooperate with the Soviets at a nuclear level by seeking a fundamental area of mutual interest: nuclear war avoidance and limitation. Thus, while appearing to stress the accommodative aspects of the Soviet-American relations, the administration was actually devising a policy that was better equipped, at least in its own opinion, to combat communism on a global scale.

NOTES

1. See Colin S. Gray, "Across the Nuclear Divide—Strategic Studies, Past and Present," *International Security* 2 (Summer 1977): 25.

2. Jerome Kahan, *Security in the Nuclear Age* (Washington, D.C.: Brookings Institution, 1975), p. 15.

3. Ibid., p. 17.

4. William W. Kaufmann, *The McNamara Strategy* (New York: Harper and Row, 1964), pp. 257-58.

5. Kahan, *Security in the Nuclear Age*, p. 73.

6. For a discussion of these and other critiques, see Harland B. Moulton, *From Superiority to Parity: The United States and the Strategic Arms Race, 1961-1971* (Westport, Conn.: Greenwood Press, 1973), pp. 27-35. See also General Maxwell D. Taylor, *The Uncertain Trumpet* (New York: Harper and Row, 1960).

7. John Foster Dulles, "Challenge and Response in United States Policy," *Foreign Affairs* 36 (October 1957): 31.

8. Edgar M. Bottome, *The Missile Gap: A Study of the Formulation of Military and Political Policy* (Teaneck, N.J.: Fairleigh Dickinson University Press, 1971), pp. 77-79.

9. See McNamara's posture statement of January 30, 1963. U.S., Arms Control and Disarmament Agency, *Documents on Disarmament, 1963*, p. 18.

10. Kaufmann, *McNamara Strategy*, p. 95.

11. Moulton, *From Superiority to Parity*, p. 51. The pledge not to use nuclear weapons first, however, was decidedly vague. For example, during the Berlin crisis of 1961, with American conventional forces not yet at full strength, Kennedy engaged in a form of brinkmanship against the Soviets. Later, during the 1962 Cuban missile crisis, the president practiced a similar form of brinkmanship.

12. Arthur M. Schlesinger, Jr., *A Thousand Days* (Boston: Houghton Mifflin, 1965; Fawcett, 1967), pp. 283-84.

13. Moulton, *From Superiority to Parity*, p. 77.

14. Seyom Brown, *The Faces of Power* (New York and London: Columbia University Press, 1968), p. 163.

15. Morton Halperin, *Defense Strategies for the Seventies* (Boston: Little, Brown, 1971), p. 50.

16. Jonathan Schell, *The Time of Illusion* (New York: Knopf, 1976), p. 94.

17. W. Averell Harriman, recorded interview conducted by Michael W. Forrestal, April 13, 1964, p. 70. John F. Kennedy Library Oral History Program.

18. U.S., President, *Public Papers of the President of the United States: John F. Kennedy* (Washington, D.C.: Government Printing Office, 1963), p. 152.

19. Kaufmann, *McNamara Strategy*, p. 103.

20. U.S., Congress, House, Committee on Armed Services, *Hearings on Military Posture*, 88th Cong., 1st sess., 1963, pp. 296-97.

21. Kaufmann, *McNamara Strategy*, p. 119.

22. Ibid., p. 116.

23. Graham T. Allison and Frederic A. Morris, "Armaments and Arms Control: Exploring the Determinants of Military Weapons," *Daedalus* 104 (Summer 1975): 99-130.

24. *Documents on Disarmament, 1963*, p. 18.

25. Allison and Morris, "Armaments and Arms Control," pp. 112-13.

26. See McNamara's testimony, U.S., Congress, Senate, Committee on Foreign Relations, *Hearings: Nuclear Test Ban Treaty*, 88th Cong., 1st sess., 1963, p. 98.

27. See McNamara's 1963 posture statement, *Documents on Disarmament, 1963*, p. 21.

28. *Hearings: Nuclear Test Ban Treaty*, pp. 100-103.

29. Ibid., p. 103.

30. Ibid., p. 104.

31. Thomas C. Schelling and Morton H. Halperin, *Strategy and Arms Control* (New York: The Twentieth Century Fund, 1961).

32. Kaufmann, *McNamara Strategy*, p. 131.

33. Ibid., p. 132.

34. Schlesinger, *A Thousand Days*, p. 442.

35. Theodore C. Sorensen, *Kennedy* (New York: Harper and Row, 1965), p. 578.

36. Mike Mansfield, recorded interview by Seth P. Tillman, June 23, 1964, p. 32. John F. Kennedy Library Oral History Program.

37. Franklin Long, "Political Implications of a Nuclear Test Ban," to President Kennedy, July 12, 1963. John F. Kennedy Library.

38. *Public Papers . . . Kennedy, 1962*, p. 899.

39. *Public Papers . . . Kennedy, 1963*, p. 602.

40. Ibid., p. 796.

41. *Hearings: Nuclear Test Ban Treaty*, pp. 792-813.

42. Ibid., p. 797.

43. Memorandum, W. W. Rostow to the Secretary of State, "The Viet Minh in Laos and the Harriman Mission," July 4, 1963; Memorandum, W. W. Rostow to the President, "The Harriman Probe," July 8, 1963, National Security Files, Box 265, John F. Kennedy Library.

44. *Public Papers . . . Kennedy, 1962*, p. 899.

45. *Public Papers . . . Kennedy, 1963*, p. 607.

46. Schlesinger, *A Thousand Days*, p. 815.

47. *Public Papers . . . Kennedy, 1963*, p. 461.

48. Ibid., p. 736.

49. Roger Hilsman, *To Move a Nation* (Garden City, N.Y.: Doubleday, 1967), p. 344.

50. See the respective testimonies of General Earle Wheeler, Admiral David L. McDonald, and General Curtis LeMay in U.S., Congress, Senate, Committee on Armed Services, Preparedness Investigating Subcommittee, *Hearings: Military Aspects and Implications of Nuclear Test Ban Treaty and Related Proposals*, 88th Cong., 1st sess., 1963, p. 676, p. 707, p. 376, respectively.

51. Memorandum, Thomas C. Hughes to Secretary of State Dean Rusk, "The Soviet View of Forthcoming Moscow Talks," June 14, 1963, p. 4, National Security Files, Box 265, John F. Kennedy Library.

52. *Newsweek*, 15 July 1963, p. 15.

53. *Public Papers . . . Kennedy, 1963*, p. 15.

54. Ibid., p. 20.

55. Ibid., p. 571.

56. Sorensen, *Kennedy*, p. 726.

57. Ibid.

58. Schlesinger, *A Thousand Days*, p. 110.

59. *Hearings: Military Aspects . . .*, p. 738.

60. Schlesinger, *A Thousand Days*, p. 110.

61. Charles E. Bohlen, recorded interview by Arthur Schlesinger, Jr., May 21, 1964, pp. 7-8. John F. Kennedy Library Oral History program.

62. Harold Macmillan, *At the End of the Day, 1961-1963* (New York: Harper and Row, 1973), p. 147.

63. U. Alexis Johnson, recorded interview by William Brubeck, 1964, p. 12. John F. Kennedy Library Oral History Program.

64. Schlesinger, *A Thousand Days*, p. 279.

65. Ibid., p. 342.

66. Llewellyn Thompson, recorded interviews by Elizabeth Donahue, March 23, 1964, and Joseph E. O'Conner, April 27, 1966, p. 36. John F. Kennedy Library Oral History Program.

4.
ARMS CONTROL AND DÉTENTE: THE EVOLUTION OF POLICY ON THE TEST BAN ISSUE, 1957–1963

The cornerstone of the emerging Soviet-American détente in 1963 was arms control. The extent to which American foreign policy had previously been governed by a deliberate determination to link the progress of arms control negotiations with the rise and decline of Cold War tensions is a matter of some question. Bernhard Bechhoefer noted that Secretary of State John Foster Dulles was profoundly skeptical of the salutary impact of arms control agreements in the absence of any significant reduction in East-West political tensions.[1]

THE EISENHOWER LEGACY

One might explain the arms control initiatives of the Eisenhower administration—such as the Atoms for Peace and Open Skies proposals, the convening of the 1958 Conference of Experts, and the decision to join test ban negotiations—as concessions to international pressure for the control of nuclear weapons. Viewing the Soviets as essentially untrustworthy yet mindful of the political value to the Kremlin of its apparent readiness to enter into negotiations, the administration had no choice but to produce an arms control position of its own. But this hesitant approach led to a policy that was, in Jacobson's and Stein's estimation, often self-contradictory and consistently burdened by qualifications that reduced its capacity to break meaningful negotiating ground.[2]

While the administration found it difficult to develop a strong test ban position once negotiations began, it was Eisenhower's leadership, according to Robert Gilpin, that moved the United States in the direction of test ban negotiations in the first

place. Gilpin contended that Eisenhower's "desire for a nuclear
test ban had become so strong by the fall of 1958 that it over-
rode both his previous position against a nuclear test ban as an
isolated step and his conviction that the United States should
not suspend testing until it had learned all it desired to learn
about nuclear weapons."[3] In Gilpin's estimation, the decisions
to engage the United States, first, in a Conference of Experts—
a decision made by the president and Dulles alone—and, second,
in test ban negotiations, represented major reversals in American
policy. These developments could not have occurred, according
to Gilpin, without Eisenhower's support of those in the administration who favored a test ban.

Clearly, by the time Kennedy entered office certain significant trends had already evolved. First, no matter Eisenhower's
uncertainties, the United States was by 1961 actively engaged
in test ban negotiations with the Soviets. This provided Kennedy
with a framework for negotiations, a policy upon which to
build, and a commitment to seek a test ban accord that tran-
scended partisan lines.

Second, the negotiations during the Eisenhower administration served to flesh out the issues dividing East and West. Clearly, the outstanding issue, once both sides agreed to explore a
test ban, was the question of inspection. The Soviets, while
initially agreeing to a system for on-site inspection, were not
willing to meet Western demands for rigorous means of monitor-
ing underground explosions. The issue was clouded by the existence of conflicting technical data. The 1958 Conference of
Experts concluded, perhaps with an excessive degree of
optimism, that effective control was indeed feasible. Subsequent American tests demonstrated, however, that high alti-
tude tests and deep underground explosions might conceivably
escape the detection capabilities outlined by the 1958 conference. Moreover, scientist Albert Latter who, along with Edward
Teller, had just published a book critical of any prospective
test ban,[4] developed the "decoupling" or "big hole" theory,
which advanced the proposition that tests could be concealed
underground by exploding nuclear devices in extremely large,
manmade cavities.

The new Western position, influenced as it was by the need
to devise a policed comprehensive ban, was that any movement
toward an agreement had to take into account the latest scientific evidence. In late 1959, following Khrushchev's visit to
Camp David, the Soviets agreed to consider the new data, and

by May 1960 it appeared that some agreement, including an atmospheric ban, an underground moratorium, a quota on inspections, and a coordinated research program, might in fact emerge. But with the collapse of the Paris summit, the Soviets renewed their insistence on the reliability of the conference's report and refused to consider the new data advanced by subsequent American discoveries. Whether the Soviets employed the Paris summit to frustrate the possibilities for accord or whether the new political tensions made an accord unacceptable to the Soviets at that time,[5] the technical requirements of inspection were obviously being portrayed by those in the United States opposed to a treaty on military and political grounds as the central difference between the two sides. The problem of establishing an inspection formula that could satisfy these objections was to become a central concern of the Kennedy administration in its formulation of a "comprehensive ban" policy and ultimately in its adoption of a "partial" ban.

The American insistence on an inspected ban could be understood as the consequence of two vastly different motivations. On the one hand there were those who favored a ban but who nevertheless would not accept an agreement that rested exclusively on Soviet gestures of goodwill. Within this group there were differences as to the scope and character of inspection requirements, but all agreed that the test ban was, at best, a positive development in Soviet-American relations and at the very least not potentially hazardous to American security interests. On the other hand there was a small but quite articulate group of scientists, government officials, and congressmen who believed that any ban would jeopardize the country's strategic standing; they seized on the inspection problem as the irreconcilable issue that would forestall any agreement. Their insistence on ironclad inspection safeguards was designed not necessarily to insure the emergence of a workable agreement but rather to make any agreement more difficult to achieve.

Robert Gilpin labeled these opposing viewpoints the "finite" and "infinite" containment schools.[6] The finite proponents assumed that it was technically feasible to limit the nuclear arms race and at the same time continue in a competitive political and military relationship with the Soviet Union. In other words, containment of Soviet power did not require the infinite expansion of American nuclear capabilities. The latter, on the other hand, argued that no inspection system could be devised that would guarantee against Soviet violations of a test ban agreement. Accordingly, the only alternative for American policymakers was an escalated weapons development program, complete with unrestricted testing. They opposed not only test ban negotiations but also the unofficial testing moratorium that lasted from 1958 until August 1961. There was another group, designated by Gilpin as the "control" school, that had little influence within the government but which, nevertheless, was fairly well-organized as an interest lobby. This group, led by scientist Linus Pauling, contended that the weapons race was directly responsible for the deterioration in Soviet-American relations. By controlling the arms spiral, went their argument, political tensions would soon dissipate.

Bechhoefer portrayed policy conflict within the Eisenhower administration in another way.[7] Eisenhower and his disarmament adviser Harold Stassen placed principal emphasis on disarmament negotiations as a means to reduce political tensions. In other words, by appearing to accept the U.S.S.R. as a legitimate state and by engaging the Soviets in disarmament negotiations, the path might be cleared for political accommodation. Dulles, on the other hand, stressed the need to mitigate political tensions as a means to create an atmosphere of trust necessary for disarmament negotiations. Bechhoefer did not believe that Dulles was opposed to disarmament per se, but the secretary of state was clearly unwilling to pursue negotiations when they threatened to create, for example, serious anxieties among America's NATO allies. Indeed, the Dulles view was transmitted to certain elements of the Kennedy administration, such as W. W. Rostow, who were somewhat hesitant about a test ban treaty because of its potentially disruptive effects on the Atlantic alliance.

The policy that developed during the latter days of the Eisenhower administration seems to have been an amalgamation of all these points of view, although the administration appears to have approached the test ban question more vigorously once Secretary Dulles's illness and subsequent death removed him from the policy-making scene. On the one hand, the United States explored possibilities for achieving a test ban. This itself represented a final reversal from the pre-1955 American position of insisting on the discussion of more ambitious forms of disarmament. Moreover, in 1959 the administration offered a partial treaty to the Soviet Union, leaving for the future talks on a comprehensive ban. But, as Jacobson and Stein noted, these initiatives were often diluted with conces-

sions to the infinite containment school.[8] Upon entering test
ban negotiations, the administration warned that the permanence of any agreement would be contingent upon the success
of other disarmament negotiations. Similarly, in offering its
partial treaty proposal, the administration, without outlining
its specifics, insisted on techniques for control. Quite clearly,
by allowing a consensus to be built behind his policy, the
president was attempting to satisfy the major viewpoints in his
administration.

Despite the apparent hesitancies in the American stance, the
policy-making process within the Eisenhower administration
served to focus policy debate on an issue that had at least some
realistic chance of negotiating success. Previous government
thinking on arms control during the Truman and Eisenhower
administrations had centered on comprehensive disarmament
measures.[9] By 1958, however, partly as a consequence of
Soviet initiatives and partly as a result of arms control negotiator
Harold Stassen's opposition to disarmament as an unrealizable
goal, the administration began debating the more realistic test
ban question. Despite initial attacks from the Joint Chiefs of
Staff, the Atomic Energy Commission, and Secretary of State
Dulles, the test ban issue indeed became a central focus of
internal policy debate. Thus, by the time Kennedy took office
the test ban had already mobilized a considerable amount of
government activity and had been framed in a manner that
made it ripe for renewed action.

Another consequence of the Eisenhower administration's
attempt to deal with the emerging test ban issue was the align-
ment of bureaucratic positions and the establishment of
bureaucratic mechanisms for consideration of the issue.
Jacobson and Stein noted that the Atomic Energy Commission
(AEC) and Department of Defense, particularly the former,
were against a test ban.[10] This could be attributed to the activism of AEC Chairman Lewis Strauss, who was notably adept
at bureaucratic infighting. According to Gilpin, after Strauss's
forced resignation in 1958 test ban opponents lost a formidable spokesman.[11] In favor of the test ban were the Department
of State—although Dulles's initial enthusiasm was rather reserved and his ultimate endorsement governed by political considerations—the Central Intelligence Agency (CIA), which saw
the inspection provision as a means by which the Soviet Union
could be opened up to greater surveillance, and the President's
Science Advisory Committee (PSAC).

The establishment of the Science Advisory Committee was an important step in institutionalizing the access of this key arms control group to the president. Until 1957, the scientific community occupied a secondary status in the executive branch. The General Advisory Committee was attached to the AEC and the Science Advisory Committee to the Office of Defense Mobilization. But in 1957, as an anxious response to the launching of the Soviet Sputnik, Eisenhower created the position of special White House assistant for science and technology and named James Killian of the Massachusetts Institute of Technology to fill the role. In addition, scientists were now attached directly to the president in the PSAC. Eisenhower also made use of special scientific task forces such as the Bethe panel, which helped move the administration toward a pro-ban stance. Indeed, at the Conference of Experts, which was so instrumental in giving test ban negotiations their initial momentum, the American delegation was comprised almost exclusively of scientists, with only a junior foreign service officer representing the Department of State.

A further organizational contribution of the Eisenhower administration was the establishment of the Committee of Principals, a high-level interagency group designed to coordinate and ultimately ratify arms control policy. Founded in August 1958, the committee was initially composed of the secretary of state as chairman, the secretary of defense, the chairman of the AEC, the director of the CIA, and the president's special adviser on science and technology. Eisenhower preferred that the committee operate as a consensus-building mechanism, obviating the need for his direct intervention in the policy-making process. Its establishment clearly demonstrated the new priority accorded arms control in the Eisenhower administration.

When Kennedy took office, he was thus aware of the positions of the various governmental agencies with an interest in arms control. More importantly, he inherited organizational machinery that would be instrumental in the fashioning of his own arms control policy. Two of these mechanisms, the special assistant for science and technology and the Committee of Principals, were to prove especially noteworthy in his administration.

Two other sources of policy input developed during the Eisenhower administration and continued to exert considerable

influence during the Kennedy era. The first and more easily
identifiable of these two sources was the British government.
It is clear that the United States under both Eisenhower and
Kennedy was sensitive to the opinions of allied and nonaligned
states. In fact, the pressure for a test ban from leading Third
World countries such as India was so great that in the context
of the global Cold War of that time, Americans had no alternative but to appear willing to negotiate an arms control agreement. At the same time, Britain, as the major Western ally and
as a fellow nuclear power, was much more directly instrumental
in the formulation of American policy. During the early 1950s,
France joined the two countries in disarmament initiatives;
the French, for example, collaborated in the Tripartite Proposal, presented to the sixth session of the United Nations General Assembly in 1951. Indeed, at times the two European
nations moved together beyond the United States in an attempt
to break the negotiating log jam as they did in May 1954 when
they introduced a bilateral disarmament initiative at Geneva.
But by the late 1950s, France had embarked on a program designed to give it independent nuclear striking power. As a consequence, it opposed rather than supported efforts to achieve
anything short of total, multilateral disarmament. By the end
of the decade, the "Western" negotiating position became
synonymous with the Anglo-American stance.

This stance was reached through active consultation and
coordination of policies. To be sure, the British appeared more
willing to take bolder initiatives, at least during the Eisenhower administration. This was no doubt a consequence of
Britain's closer proximity to the potential war theater and the
very active pressure of a vigorous "ban the bomb" movement
at home. At the same time, the British enjoyed easy access to
American policy-making circles, and in one dramatic instance,
Prime Minister Harold Macmillan himself flew to Washington
to prod the American administration into being more forthcoming at the negotiating table. Differences notwithstanding,
it is clear that the British were active and generally welcome
participants in the American policy-making process.

A much less clearly defined source of influence was the
domestic political environment. According to Jacobson and
Stein, public interest in test ban negotiations was relatively
episodic, rising in relation to dramatic events such as the Soviet
moratorium violation but by and large quiescent.[12] Neverthe-

less, policymakers did not operate in a political vacuum. During the 1956 presidential campaign, Democratic presidential candidate Adlai Stevenson prodded Eisenhower to respond to his proposal for a unilateral disarmament initiative. In addition, numerous scientists and public interest groups such as the Committee for a Sane Nuclear Policy (SANE) made a strong case for the suspension of nuclear testing, while respected members of the foreign policy establishment, such as George Kennan, were suggesting means for the amelioration of tensions in Europe through such measures as mutual disengagement.

By far, the greatest source of influence came from individual congressmen using legislative machinery to press their own viewpoints on the administration. During the Eisenhower era, the foremost Democratic spokesman in favor of a test ban was Senator Hubert Humphrey of Minnesota, who employed his Subcommittee on Disarmament to incubate the test ban issue. Another Democrat, Senator Albert Gore of Tennessee, who had observed the negotiations in Geneva firsthand, was chary of a comprehensive pact, but he is credited with being the first major American political figure to recommend an atmospheric ban. With the administration unsettled about the course of American policy, these voices were accorded greater value than might otherwise have been the case. In a sense, Congress assumed a policy-initiation role during the Eisenhower administration.

In summary, upon taking power in January 1961, the Kennedy administration walked into a policy area that had already developed considerable momentum of its own. To be sure, by 1961 East-West negotiations were profoundly deadlocked. Nevertheless, events during the Eisenhower administration had committed the United States to search for a workable test ban accord. A negotiating framework had been established, central issues had been drawn, and interested parties, from within and outside the executive branch, had been mobilized. Kennedy's task upon assuming power was, therefore, twofold. First, employing the policy-making machinery available to him, the new president had to seek a formula that would move the negotiations off dead center. Second, he would have to sustain and even build support outside the executive branch in the face of continued Soviet obstructionism within the context of a strong public anti-Soviet mood. These related tasks were ultimately to occupy a considerable portion of his interest, time, and political energy.

KENNEDY'S FIRST TWO YEARS:
ORGANIZING FOR ARMS CONTROL

The Eisenhower administration left office with the test ban
negotiations stalemated and Soviet-American relations in a
general state of decline. Having pledged during the campaign
to attach a high priority to arms control,[13] the new president
began his tenure by ordering an administration-wide review of
the American negotiating position. This review resulted in a
draft treaty, which was tabled by the United States at the
Geneva conference on April 18, 1961. While the American
position was only marginally different from previous Western
proposals, it represented the first time that any administration
had presented a full draft treaty for consideration. Despite outright Soviet rejection of the treaty, the president instructed
Ambassador Arthur Dean to propose a concession on the
inspection issue by offering the Soviets a sliding scale from
twelve to twenty inspections per year. The rejection of this concession demonstrated that a wide gulf still divided East and
West on the central inspection issue. It also represented one
hint among several that the Soviets were about to abrogate the
testing moratorium.

The moratorium was a collateral but no less significant issue.
The Joint Chiefs, along with several influential members of
Congress and the scientific community, were hectoring the
president to resume underground testing, even before the Soviet
atmospheric explosion of August 1961. As a response to this
pressure, the president convened the blue-ribbon Panofsky
panel, named after its chairman Wolfgang Panofsky, to evaluate the potential for Soviet duplicity and to make recommendations regarding the advisability of renewed American testing.
The panel, organized under the auspices of the PSAC, acknowledged that the Soviets could have cheated, but it found no evidence
to support the contention that in fact they had. More importantly, the panel saw little value in the resumption of American
testing. The president, sympathetic to its conclusions, sided
with the Panofsky panel and refused to initiate a testing program
until after the Soviets had resumed one of their own. Even
then he began with the authorization of underground tests and
ordered the resumption of atmospheric testing only after the
talks showed little sign of leading to a breakthrough.

The president's determination to avoid the unilateral resumption of nuclear testing and at the same time to achieve a semblance of momentum at Geneva, was facilitated by his approach to the management of the executive branch.[14] This approach was in large part a reaction to the cumbersome policy machinery developed by his predecessor. Eisenhower, whose military background led him to inflated expectations about the efficacy of a clearly delineated chain of command, used what Clark and Legere called a "formalized codification" approach.[15] The president was interested in reconciling policy with action. To insure this, policy was clearly enunciated in an annual series of National Security Policy Papers. The purpose of these papers was to apprise lower-level bureaucrats of the administration's policies. To guarantee the execution of policy, Eisenhower established within the National Security Council (NSC) an Operations Coordinating Board which issued periodic "Action Status Reports" designed to monitor the responsiveness of the foreign policy bureaucracy. Broad policy, however, was made by the NSC's planning board, composed of the assistant secretaries of the council's constituent agencies and departments. In addition to the NSC, the cabinet was revived as a significant policy-making organ. Periodic meetings between the cabinet secretary and the "cabinet assistants," a group of assistant secretaries from cabinet-level departments, were also used to monitor the implementation of cabinet decisions within the various bureaucracies.

When Kennedy assumed the presidency, he was determined to reduce the number of boards and agencies, which had multiplied under Eisenhower's "pyramidal" system of management. The new president reasoned that instead of aiding him in asserting control over the government, the coordinating boards tended to insulate the chief executive from the hub of the decision-making process. Based on the advice of reorganization advisers such as presidential scholar Richard Neustadt, Kennedy dismantled the boards, abolished the cabinet secretariat, and de-emphasized the role of the cabinet. To monitor government operations, the new president relied on two strategies. First, he employed the National Security Council, and particularly its chief McGeorge Bundy, as a personal staff rather than an interagency decision-making board. One of the major criticisms leveled at the Eisenhower NSC was its propensity to produce "watered-down" recommendations resulting from the need to satisfy the variety of interests and viewpoints represented on the council. Under Eisenhower, a premium was

placed on the achievement of consensus prior to presidential
decision. This was a major reason for the construction of so
many coordinating boards, and it describes Eisenhower's use
of the Committee of Principals. But Kennedy, according to
the then deputy under secretary of state for political affairs,
U. Alexis Johnson, "wanted to get things done before they
had become too orderly, before opinions had become too com-
partmentalized."[16] Second, and perhaps more importantly,
the president, in order to achieve a greater harmony between
policy and action, attempted as much as possible to monitor
the implementation of decisions himself. To do so, he established contacts with lower-level bureaucrats, thereby hoping
to circumvent routine channels of command. As Louis Koenig
wrote, Kennedy tried to build administration-wide personal
relationships rather than institutions.[17]

Kennedy's approach has been widely labeled as "action"
rather than "policy" oriented. This description has been used
to distinguish his administration from Eisenhower's. The
Eisenhower model assumed that a hierarchical system would
automatically convert broad policy into specific action.
Kennedy, apparently more attuned to the vagaries of the bureaucratic process, eschewed broad policy declarations as futile. Instead, he approached each issue from an action perspective and
organized special interagency task forces to deal with them.
According to this pragmatic decision-making model, policy
"tended to be viewed more as a set of reasons lying behind an
action program undertaken, or simply as a description of an
action program; the action itself was the focus of interest."[18]

Kennedy's informal approach to decision making was con-
trived to encourage presidential control over the policy-making
process. Nevertheless, it too had certain inherent limitations.
First, it placed a great premium on active presidential involvement in the development of policy. According to presidential
adviser Charles Bohlen, Kennedy might have, in fact, been
"somewhat overimpressed by [Richard] Neustadt's book on
the power of the President in that a strong President always
went outside channels."[19] While this emphasis on the employment of personal presidential power paid dividends in areas
where the president chose to exercise his influence, it inevitably
allowed for greater bureaucratic independence in other areas.
Second, the creation of ad hoc panels did not obviate the need
for intra-administration consensus building. Instead of con-
structing consensus through formal institutions such as the

National Security Council or cabinet, the mechanisms for
bureaucratic infighting were the informal boards and panels.
As Adrian Fisher, deputy director of the Arms Control and
Disarmament Agency during the Kennedy administration,
noted, the Joint Chiefs of Staff, who had strong reservations
about the comprehensive ban that Kennedy favored, were
actively involved in the interagency planning that led to the
American proposals of August 1962.[20] That these deliberations were conducted under the ad hoc auspices of the ACDA
did not mean that this important and sometimes vexatious
group was excluded from the decision-making process.

These limitations notwithstanding, the evolution of the administration's policy in 1961-62 resulted in a coherent arms
control position—a quality singularly lacking in the Eisenhower
administration. This coherence can be attributed to three factors.
First, Kennedy chose arms control as an area of principal personal concern and involvement. Second, the president filled
key administration posts with individuals who had contributed
to theory building in the arms control movement. Finally, the
establishment of a new arms control coordinating unit, the
Arms Control and Disarmament Agency, aided the president in
asserting control over his administration in this key issue area.

In August 1962, Ambassador Dean tabled two draft treaties
at Geneva, one proposing a comprehensive, the other a partial,
ban. As Fisher remembered, the idea for a limited ban did not
originate with the president;[21] rather, its key administration
exponents were John McNaughton of the Defense Department
and Carl Kaysen of the National Security Council.[22] Under the
direction of the ACDA, the 1962 arms control reevaluation
involved a major executive branch consensus-building project.
Upon concluding its final meeting on July 3, the interagency
task force sent the two drafts to relevant agencies for final comment. On July 20 the Committee of Principal's Committee of
Deputies met to discuss the new viewpoints. As a consequence,
two revised drafts were composed. These drafts were submitted to the Committee of Principals on July 26. Only then
were they submitted to the president for his consideration and
formal authorization.

The attempt to build a consensus behind the "two-draft" proposal did not occur, however, without significant presidential
participation. Fisher recalled that the president was well aware
of the interagency group's decision to consider a limited ban
and made his opinions known through constant questioning
and prodding. He was also apprised of the scientific develop-

ments that led to a review of the administration's position on
a comprehensive ban and informed a press conference in July
1962, ". . . we've been attempting . . . to bring our own position in line with new scientific data available to us since late
June."[23] According to Fisher, ". . . [Kennedy] seemed to me
about as well advised on the subject as any non-scientific person could be."[24]

In addition, Kennedy used the Committee of Principals to
exert considerable influence on the shaping of policy. The
committee, which met eleven times between March 1 and
August 1, 1962, was supplied with firm presidential guidelines,
unlike the deliberations of the committee during the Eisenhower administration. As it was a high-level interagency group,
these guidelines were communicated downward to those areas
of the bureaucracy involved in staff work. Finally, once the
task force's recommendations were made known to the president, the Committee of Principals met with him two additional
times, on July 30 and August 1.

Kennedy's interest in promoting a strong arms control position was conveyed to his administration not only through active
presidential involvement in the policy-making process but by
the placement of like-minded personnel in important decision-
making posts. According to Abram Chayes, legal adviser to the
State Department under Kennedy, men such as Jerome Wiesner,
Arthur Schlesinger, Jr., and Carl Kaysen were interested in exploring new directions in East-West relations.[25] Schlesinger
credited Wiesner, who became the president's scientific
adviser, with keeping the arms control initiative alive in the
executive branch.[26] During the 1960 campaign, Wiesner had
written an article for *Daedalus* in which he criticized the West
for its timidity on the disarmament issue.[27] Shortly after the
1960 election, Wiesner attended the Pugwash conference and
became convinced that the Soviets were indeed serious about
achieving a test ban agreement. He carried this impression with
him in his new post as the president's special assistant for science and technology. Another major personnel change, according to Jacobson and Stein, was the replacement of hard-line
AEC Chairman John McCone with Glenn Seaborg.[28] At the
department level, Secretary of Defense Robert McNamara was
valued not only for his ability to control the military, but for
recognizing that he could only "go so far in overwhelming the
Joint Chiefs of Staff if he was to maintain morale and support
within the Pentagon."[29]

At the center of the administration's arms control activity

in 1961-62 was the newly formed Arms Control and Disarmament Agency. According to Sorensen, the agency was established because Kennedy felt that too little governmental attention was being devoted to the subject of arms control.[30] Indeed, while many government organizations were involved to some degree in the formulation of arms control policy, the only governmental unit devoting full-time attention to the problem was the relatively small Disarmament Administration situated in the Department of State. The creation of the agency also signaled the administration's public determination to make progress in this area. An outgrowth of the Democratic Advisory Council's "Peace Agency" idea, it satisfied the liberal wing of Kennedy's party, which had made arms control a high-priority item in the Democratic platform.

The most important function of the ACDA was to give the president greater control over the arms control efforts of his administration. Richard Neustadt, who along with Republican John McCloy was one of the architects of the new agency, was interested in making it as responsive to the president as bureaucratically feasible. In a memo to McCloy, he suggested that the unit should be a "self-contained administrative entity headed by a Director who ranks bureaucratically with the Under Secretary of State and Deputy Secretary of Defense."[31] More importantly, he preferred that the head of the agency report directly to the president rather than through the secretary of state, and consequently the ACDA represented a bureaucratic anomaly. While nominally under the authority of the secretary of state—who as the principal foreign policy adviser in the administration had first claim to the formulation of arms control policy—the agency director was, in a very real sense, directly answerable to the president. In the hands of a president with great interest in arms control the ACDA could, therefore, be a powerful mechanism for political control. This feature was accentuated by Trevor Gardner, assistant secretary of defense for research and development under Eisenhower and originator of the Peace Agency idea, in testimony before the Senate Foreign Relations Committee:

> I believe that the organization will work as long as the President retains a strong and continuing interest in the disarmament area. . . . I would think that in the event we had a President whose interest was not strong in that area

that the two-headed facet of reporting might be a de-
ficiency.[32]

During the 1962 review of the administration's test ban policy
the agency and its director William Foster assumed the principal coordinating role within the executive branch. This was, in
part, a consequence of the agency's preference for a comprehensive ban, a preference shared by the president. It was also a
function of the president's greater interest in arms control and
Secretary of State Dean Rusk's relative diffidence on the issue.[33]
With access to a wide array of government agencies and research
facilities outside the government, the ACDA's task forces considered all proposals and prepared them for review by the Committee of Principals. These functions within the government
were matched by sedulous ACDA efforts to cultivate congressional opinion and by its coordination of all government public
information programs.

By the late summer of 1962, the administration, despite continued Soviet intransigence on the issue, had fashioned a test
ban policy that satisfied major governmental interests. The hard
liners, particularly among the military, were at least temporarily
reconciled by the continued American insistence on verified
inspection and by the resumption of atmospheric testing. The
comprehensive ban advocates, particularly in the ACDA, were
encouraged by the determination of the administration to continue the search for a treaty prohibiting underground testing.
A middle ground was struck by the simultaneous proposal of a
partial ban, a proposal that the president did not necessarily
favor but that nevertheless won his approval. In retrospect,
Kennedy's decision to permit the tabling over the objections
of his arms control experts in the ACDA of a partial ban
cleared the path for an agreement that would satisfy both
the Soviet Union and his domestic critics.

Soviet-American relations failed to improve at the beginning
of Kennedy's administration. In fact, with the American involvement in Viet Nam escalating, the resumption of nuclear testing on both sides, and the ever-worsening Berlin crisis, one
might argue that relations had deteriorated even further, reaching a nadir with the Cuban missile crisis of October. Nevertheless,
the Kennedy administration ranked arms control as a high-
priority foreign policy item. One reason was, as already stated,
the prominence of the military collaboration doctrine in the
upper reaches of the administration. According to this line of

thought, continued conflict with the Soviet Union and its client states did not rule out the achievement of some stability in the "balance of terror."

Perhaps even more important in moving the administration toward the development of a coherent arms control policy was the president's willingness and ability to involve himself in the decision-making process. Eisenhower was deeply troubled by the arms race, but he did not have a concept of presidential power that would lead to the assertion of his will over a divided administration. Kennedy, whose interest in arms control was more pragmatic than Eisenhower's, was, on the other hand, willing to flex his political muscle within the executive branch and even beyond. He did this by active presidential involvement in the policy-making process, by placing arms control advocates in key government positions, and by employing the ACDA as an arms control coordinating unit. This activism did not immediately produce an arms accord, but it did produce an arms control policy.

THE ROAD TO A TREATY: TEST BAN NEGOTIATIONS IN 1963

The negotiating tempo accelerated dramatically following the denouement of the Cuban missile crisis. During the crisis, the president and the Soviet premier had exchanged letters expressing the need for progress on a test ban. On December 19, 1962, Chairman Khrushchev forwarded a personal letter to President Kennedy in which he offered to accept a limit of three on-site inspections per year as part of a comprehensive pact. In advancing these concessions, the Soviet premier relied on conversations between Ambassadors Dean and V. V. Kuznetsov and scientists Wiesner and Yevgenii Federov in which the Americans were alleged to have agreed that three inspections would be sufficient. Khrushchev adhered to the Soviet position that internationally supervised inspections were unnecessary, but he acknowledged that the exigencies of congressional endorsement were factors in softening the Soviet stand, a theme that would recur throughout subsequent negotiations.[34]

Kennedy, in his response, attempted to clarify the American position by first rejecting the Soviet understanding of the Dean-Wiesner exercises in personal diplomacy. The president also made a point of affirming that his insistence on a greater number of on-site inspections was a consequence of American security interests rather than anticipated Congressional reactions.[35] Nevertheless, Kennedy struck a positive note in his letter and recommended the immediate convening of a high-level tripartite conference in New York and Washington.

The impending negotiations were accompanied by a positive American gesture. On January 26, 1963, the president postponed the planned detonation of an underground nuclear explosion that had been scheduled for as early as January 1. The new momentum, however, failed to produce a significant narrowing of Soviet-American differences on the inspection issue. The Soviets stuck to their interpretation of the Dean-Wiesner "concessions," while the United States and Britain continued to insist that three inspections were not sufficient safeguards against Soviet cheating.[36] As a consequence of the renewed stalemate, the president decided to resume underground testing, and the talks shifted once again to the eighteen-nation Geneva conference.

Despite their disappointment, comprehensive ban advocates within the administration were persistent in their search for a formula that would break the logjam. McNamara was willing to accept six as the minimum number of inspections that would guarantee against surreptitious Soviet violations. Wiesner, who was perhaps the most active of the comprehensive ban advocates within the administration, would have accepted five. According to Schlesinger, "The President was particularly interested in the possibility of lowering the required quota of annual on-site inspections from the existing figure of twenty. Spurred on by presidential concern, scientists worked to refine techniques of identifications and inspection."[37] Despite growing and more vocal congressional clamor against possible American concessions, in February and March the administration reformulated its negotiating position to allow for a minimum number of seven inspections and modified its requirements regarding the character of the inspection teams. But this offer, as controversial as it was in Congress, did little to soften the Soviet stand; instead, the Soviet negotiators continued to press for a maximum of three inspections, while Khrushchev stepped up his truculent attacks against the Western position.[38] Moreover, in April the Soviets initiated a diplomatic offensive against the American proposal to provide NATO countries with nuclear weapons under the MLF scheme.[39] Kennedy was becoming increasingly pessimistic, but he continued to attach high priority to the achievement of a test ban agreement. Failure to reach an accord in the near future would, in the president's own words, let the "genie out of the bottle."[40]

In April positive developments in two collateral negotiating areas—one involving the creation of a direct communications link between Moscow and Washington and the other setting up a weather inspection exchange between the two countries— signaled some progress in relations. Nevertheless, the elusive inspection issue continued to stymie the test ban negotiations. As part of a British initiative to salvage the negotiations, the United States agreed to send the Soviets a note proposing the convening of a high-level meeting in Moscow. Later that spring, on May 27, thirty-four senators, including Senator Thomas Dodd of Connecticut and Senator Hubert Humphrey, passed a resolution recommending that the United States actively seek an accord to prohibit nuclear testing in the atmosphere and under the sea.

New momentum was generated by both sides when, on June 8, Premier Khrushchev agreed to convene the Moscow conference. In response, Kennedy announced the unilateral American commitment not to be the first nation to resume atmospheric testing, and on June 10 in an address delivered at American University the president appeared to accept the Soviet doctrine of "peaceful co-existence." The impending conference generated a high-level interdepartmental review of the British-American negotiating position. This review led to two major decisions, each reflecting a large measure of presidential input. First, the president chose Ambassador Averell Harriman, a strong advocate of a nuclear test ban, as the chairman of the American delegation. Second, the administration, reflecting Kennedy's continued preference for a pact outlawing all forms of nuclear testing, decided to press for a comprehensive ban in Moscow.

The Soviet response to the Western initiative was generally favorable. The president's speech was beamed throughout the Soviet Union. Moreover, in an interview published in the Soviet press, Premier Khrushchev welcomed the message contained in the American University address.[41] While he objected to the continued ambivalences in American policy, specifically with regard to Berlin and the issue of a nonagression pact for Europe, the Soviet premier regarded the president's remarks as a great step forward. Indeed a year later, following Kennedy's death, Khrushchev took special note of the president address: "That statement can be called courageous and more realistic than what the Soviet Union and other countries of the socialist world often heard from American leaders."[42] With Khrushchev's July 2 announcement that the Soviet Union would now be willing to engage in a partial ban and with the apparent collapse of Sino-Soviet high-level discussions one week later, the stage was set for an agreement on a limited pact.[43]

Despite some negotiating difficulties in Moscow, delegates from the three nuclear states initialed the treaty on July 25. Defended by the president as the "product of the steady effort of the United States Government in two administrations"[44] and portrayed as being vital to the national interest, the administration submitted the treaty for Senate ratification on August 8. Upon the conclusion of extensive hearings, the Senate Foreign Relations Committee, the committee with principal responsibility for advising the full Senate on treaties, recommended ratification. On September 24 the Senate, voting in a bipartisan fashion, ratified the Nuclear Test Ban Treaty, 80 to 19.

NOTES

1. Bernhard G. Bechhoefer, *Postwar Negotiations for Arms Control* (Washington, D.C.: Brookings Institution, 1961), p. 429.

2. Harold Karan Jacobson and Eric Stein, *Diplomats, Scientists and Politicians: The United States and the Nuclear Test Ban Negotiations* (Ann Arbor, Mich.: The University of Michigan Press, 1966), pp. 471-73.

3. Robert Gilpin, *American Scientists and Nuclear Weapons Policy* (Princeton, N.J.: Princeton University Press, 1962), p. 196.

4. Edward Teller and Albert Latter, *Our Nuclear Future: Dangers and Opportunities* (New York: Criterion Books, 1958).

5. "Kremlin leaders seemed to view negotiations mainly as a means of disguising the USSR's military deficiencies, acquiring prestige through the illusion of sincerity, and reducing the risk of U.S. attack as they slowly built a reliable deterrent." Jerome Kahan, *Security in the Nuclear Age* (Washington, D.C.: Brookings Institution, 1975), p. 61.

6. Gilpin, *American Scientists*, pp. 66-107.

7. Bechhoefer, *Postwar Negotiations*, pp. 429-35.

8. Jacobson and Stein, *Diplomats, Scientists and Politicians*, p. 472.

9. See William R. Frye, "The Quest for Disarmament Since World War II," in *Arms Control: Issues for the Public*, ed. Louis Henkin (Englewood Cliffs, N.J.: Prentice-Hall, 1961), pp. 18-48.

10. Jacobson and Stein, *Diplomats, Scientists, and Politicians*, p. 471. See also George B. Kistiakowsky, *A Scientist at the White House* (Cambridge, Mass.: Harvard University Press, 1976).

11. Gilpin, *American Scientists*, p. 199.

12. Jacobson and Stein, *Diplomats, Scientists, and Politicians*, p. 470.

13. U.S., Arms Control and Disarmament Agency, *Documents on Disarmament, 1960*, p. 289.

14. The material covering the organizational approaches of the Eisenhower and Kennedy presidencies borrows from the following works: Keith C. Clark and Laurence J. Legere, *The President and the Management of National Security* (New York: Praeger, 1969); I. M. Destler,

Presidents, Bureaucrats and Foreign Policy (Princeton, N.J.: Princeton University Press, 1972); Richard Tanner Johnson, *Managing the White House: An Intimate Study of the Presidency* (New York: Harper and Row, 1974); Louis Koenig, *The Chief Executive* (New York: Harcourt, Brace and World, 1968).

15. Clark and Legere, *The President and National Security*, p. 217.

16. U. Alexis Johnson, recorded interview by William Brubeck, 1964, pp. 13-15. John F. Kennedy Library Oral History Program.

17. Koenig, *The Chief Executive*, p. 172.

18. Clark and Legere, *The President and National Security*, p. 72.

19. Charles Bohlen, recorded interview by Arthur M. Schlesinger, Jr., May 21, 1964, p. 30. John F. Kennedy Library Oral History Program.

20. Adrian Fisher, recorded interview by Frank Sieverts, May 13, 1964, p. 14. John F. Kennedy Library Oral History Program.

21. Ibid.

22. Arthur M. Schlesinger, Jr., *A Thousand Days* (Boston: Houghton Mifflin, 1965; Fawcett, 1967), p. 456.

23. U.S., President, *Public Papers of the Presidents of the United States* (Washington, D.C.: U.S. Government Printing Office, 1963), John F. Kennedy, 1962, p. 592.

24. Fisher interview, p. 15.

25. Abram Chayes, recorded interviews by Eugene Gordon, May 18, 1964; June 22, 1964; June 23, 1964, p. 226. John F. Kennedy Library Oral History Program.

26. Schlesinger, *A Thousand Days*, p. 465.

27. Jerome B. Wiesner, "Comprehensive Arms Limitation Systems," *Daedalus* 89 (Fall 1960): 917-18.

28. Jacobson and Stein, *Diplomats, Scientists, and Politicians*, p. 270.

29. Theodore Sorensen, recorded interview by Carl Kaysen, March 26, 1964, and April 4, 1964, p. 14. John F. Kennedy Library Oral History Program.

30. Theodore C. Sorensen, *Kennedy* (New York: Harper and Row, 1965), p. 578.

31. Memorandum, Richard Neustadt to John J. McCloy re: Location of the contemplated disarmament organization, March 29, 1961, President's Office Files, Box 36, John F. Kennedy Library.

32. U.S., Congress, Senate, Committee on Foreign Relations, *Hearings: Disarmament Agency-S, 2180-A Bill to Establish a United States Disarmament Agency for World Peace and Security*, 87th Cong., 1st sess., 1961, p. 195.

33. Schlesinger, *A Thousand Days*, p. 466.

34. This concern was expressed most pointedly by Premier Khruschchev in discussions with peace activist Norman Cousins, *The Improbable Triumvirate* (New York: Norton, 1972), p. 96.

35. *Documents on Disarmament, 1962*, 2 vols., 2: 1277-79.

36. See Secretary of State Rusk's news conference of February 1, 1963. *Documents on Disarmament, 1963*, pp. 28-29.

37. Schlesinger, *A Thousand Days*, pp. 816-19.

38. See Khrushchev's interview with the Italian newspaper *Il Giorno*, April 20, 1963. *Documents on Disarmament, 1963*, pp. 173-76.

39. *Documents on Disarmament, 1963*, pp. 161-70.

40. *Public Papers . . . Kennedy, 1963*, p. 424.

41. *Documents on Disarmament, 1963*, pp. 222-28.

42. Nikita Khrushchev, oral history interview conducted on June 29, 1964, p. 2. John F. Kennedy Library Oral History Program.

43. The extent of the differences between the two Communist giants became apparent on July 31, 1963, when Peking Radio launched a bitter diatribe against the Soviet initiative. *Documents on Disarmament, 1963*, pp. 268-72.

44. *Documents on Disarmament, 1963*, p. 302.

5.
THE TEST BAN TREATY
AND THE POLICY-MAKING
PROCESS

Assessing President Kennedy's role in reaching agreement with the Soviet Union on a limited test ban, National Security Adviser McGeorge Bundy commented less than one year after the president's death:

> Unless the President uses these powers with energy, arms control agreements are improbable. The momentum of the arms race—the power at work to keep it going almost without conscious new decisions—is enormous. Military men in all countries find it hard to approve any arms control proposal which is not either safely improbable or clearly unbalanced in their favor. In the United States only a strong Commander-in-Chief with a strong Secretary of Defense is in a position to press steadily for recognition that the arms race itself is now a threat to national security. Only the President can ensure that good proposals are kept alive even after a first rejection, and that new possibilities are constantly considered—so that there may always be as many proposals as possible on the table waiting for the moment of Soviet readiness.[1]

The successful negotiation and ratification of the Test Ban Treaty appear to confirm Bundy's assessment of the end product of presidential determination to employ power in behalf of arms control initiatives. Indeed, if the Kennedy administration is an example of this rule in operation, then the Eisenhower presidency is perhaps representative of the reverse. Despite the existence of bureaucratic forces in favor of a test ban and the president's own latent preference for an end to the arms spiral, Eisenhower's failure to assert himself more vigorously within his administration led to the pursuit of rather unclear policy objectives. If Bundy's argument is taken to its logical conclusion, then one might speculate that had Eisenhower been more determined in pressing for the development of a coherent test ban policy, a treaty might have been initialed before Kennedy came to the presidency.

Nevertheless, the potential for irresolution was present in the Kennedy administration. The principal source of governmental opposition to Kennedy's test ban efforts was the Joint Chiefs of Staff. To be sure, civilian elements of the administration did not always agree about specific arms control measures. For example, following the Soviet abrogation of the testing moratorium in August 1961, Secretary of State Rusk recommended the immediate resumption of above-ground testing, while Edward R. Murrow, director of the U.S. Information Agency (USIA), among others, recommended against testing by arguing that such a move would rob the Soviet violation of its intrinsic political value to the United States. In 1962 with the administration formulating a new approach to the Geneva negotiations, the ACDA was reluctant to go along with the decision to offer a partial treaty as an alternative proposal, lest it appear to dilute the administration's stated resolve to negotiate a comprehensive pact. From the other end of the policy spectrum, W. W. Rostow of the National Security Council (NSC) expressed strong reservations about the administration's determination to take advantage of Khrushchev's apparent change of heart and negotiate a three-environment ban.[2]

Tactical differences aside, the civilian sector of the administration, from the secretaries of state and defense to the director of the CIA, were in basic accord regarding the value of a test ban agreement. According to Benjamin Read, under Rusk the executive secretary of the Department of State, the effort to win congressional support for the Test Ban Treaty entailed "tremendous unanimity among those involved."[3]

The military's objections to the arms control measures of the Kennedy administration stemmed, however, from a fundamental skepticism about arms control as a concept. This does not mean that the Joint Chiefs were united in the degree of their opposition; it is possible, for example, to place Chairman Maxwell D. Taylor, sympathetic to Kennedy's strategic thinking, at one end of the spectrum, and Curtis LeMay of the air force at the other end. As LeMay himself acknowledged in testimony before the Senate, "I am less optimistic than other members of the Joint Chiefs on this particular subject."[4] Nevertheless, it is doubtful that the military as a group would have recommended the test ban on their own initiative. Instead, the story of the administration's test ban efforts points to the exertion of tremendous civilian pressure in bringing the military into line. Their ultimate endorsement of a limited test ban reflects both the relatively innocent character of the treaty and their grudging acceptance of political realities.

In part, one might explain the military point of view as a consequence of its adherents' role perceptions. According to Samuel P. Huntington, one of the foremost experts on civilian-military relations, the military's functional role of national security maintenance compels it to overemphasize the immediate threat to that security.[5] Because of their sense of professional responsibility, military men, according to Huntington, assume the "worst case" and calculate that overestimating the degree of external threat is safer than underestimating it. This is translated into a general assumption that as long as another country possesses a significant military capability, there is always a danger that it will be used.

Kennedy had attempted earlier in his administration to induce the military people to reach beyond their narrow, professional outlooks in offering their recommendations to him. In a National Security Action Memorandum (NSAM) circulated to the Joint Chiefs in mid-1961, the president urged the military, particularly in matters pertaining to the Cold War, to take into account political considerations.[6] He repeated this theme directly to the Joint Chiefs while attempting to win them over to a limited test ban some two years later.[7] Nevertheless, in their defense of the Test Ban Treaty on Capitol Hill, the service chiefs continued to distinguish between, rather than to synthesize, military and political concerns. Testifying before the Senate Foreign Relations Committee, LeMay acknowledged that political rather than military considerations had been instrumental in gaining Joint Chiefs' support for the treaty. "I would say probably the key factor was political in this case. We examined the military and the technical aspects and came up with a net disadvantage in that field."[8]

Civilian officials, such as Kennedy, McNamara, and McNaughton, believed that arms control could serve to maintain a favorable military balance between the United States and the U.S.S.R. One of the principal administration arguments in support of a comprehensive ban was that continued testing on both sides might undermine America's nuclear superiority, especially because the Soviets had yet to learn all that was possible from underground testing.[9] But the military argued that a policy of arms control would ultimately jeopardize national security by placing too much trust in the Soviets' inclination to restrain their nuclear policies. Thomas J. Power, under Kennedy the commander of the Strategic Air Command, testified against Senate ratification of the Test Ban Treaty in these words: "I believe that it is a mistake to maintain any posture other than that of overwhelming military superiority."[10] Other air force representatives were equally harsh in their assessment of Kennedy's policies. In early 1963, *The New York Times* quoted several air force sources to the effect that the administration was willing to settle for a nuclear "stalemate" with the Soviet Union.[11] On September 11, 1963, during the height of the Senate debate over ratification of the Test Ban Treaty, the Air Force Association approved a policy statement charging Kennedy with adopting a "nuclear stalemate strategy."[12]

In a similar vein, Admiral George Anderson, whose position as navy Chief of Staff was not renewed as of July 1963, testified before the Preparedness Investigating Subcommittee:

> . . . United States must maintain a clear military superiority, including nuclear striking power over the Communist bloc in order that the penalty of military aggression on the part of the Communists will be obvious, it will be certain, it will be prompt, and as devasting as necessary to the Communists if they resort to any form of aggression.[13]

Both civilian and military officials agreed that the American military posture should be one of nuclear superiority. Civilian officials, however, believed that superiority could be stabilized by arms control measures and assumed that a military understanding between the United States and the U.S.S.R. carried with it an implicit acknowledgment on both sides of American nuclear superiority. The military, however, did not believe that the Soviets could be trusted to restrain themselves in the realm of nuclear weapons. Political agreements might lead to a relaxation of tensions, but they could not be expected to influence Soviet nuclear policy. In fact, this point of view was the exact

reverse of the arms control thinking of the civilian elements of
the administration. The latter believed that whereas political
tensions might continue, there was room for accommodation
in the realm of military strategy. The military, however, argued
that whereas agreements might conceivably lead to a relaxation
of political tensions, only unilateral, unfettered weapons development could possibly deter Soviet might. It is clear, therefore,
that while civilian elements of the administration by and large
saw an intrinsic strategic value in arms control agreements, the
Joint Chiefs of Staff viewed arms control as being of limited
military value if not an outright detriment to the strategic
standing of the nation.[14]

It is difficult to gauge the extent to which the military point
of view was, in fact, instrumental in the development of the
American arms control position. It is clear that the decision
to follow the Soviet abrogation of the unofficial testing moratorium with the resumption of underground and atmospheric
testing bore a strong military imprint. It is also clear that interagency consideration of the American negotiating stance invariably produced some provision that appeared to take into
account strongly held military reservations. For example, the
revised American proposals of March 23, 1963, contained a
measure designed to satisfy the military's insistence on the
right of withdrawal from a comprehensive treaty.[15]

At the same time, there was ongoing tension between civilian
and military officials over the test ban issue—a tension in no
small part traceable to the strained relationship then existing
between the Joint Chiefs of Staff and Secretary of Defense
McNamara. In some respects, their conflict reflected a fundamental division regarding perceptions of the Soviet threat.
As one aide to the Joint Chiefs of Staff confided to journalist
Marvin Kalb in the 1960s, "McNamara thinks that the Russian
Chiefs reason the way we do. Well, from our point of view
that's madness."[16] Bureaucratic politics were also to blame for
the split. According to Herbert York, the military resented the
secretary's intrusion into areas that were traditionally considered to be within their pale of expertise.[17] Several of the
chiefs believed that they were deliberately being frozen out of
the policy-making process. Throughout 1963 the McNamara-
Joint Chiefs imbroglio captured national headlines. On April
20 the secretary of defense saw fit to respond to his military
critics by asserting that *he* was in the best position to deter-
mine the nation's security needs.[18] The administration's de-

cision to affix its signature to the Moscow treaty did not
reduce the strain. In September Admiral Anderson, by then
a former member of the Joint Chiefs, accused McNamara of
downgrading military advice.[19] On October 4 Louisiana
Representative F. Edward Hebert, a staunch military ally on
Capitol Hill, charged that civilians in the Defense Department
were meddling in military affairs.[20]

But McNamara, although the most visible protagonist in the
continuing round of civilian-military jousting, was not the only
civilian official to be skeptical about the military's ability to
provide reasoned and objective policy recommendations.
According to those close to the president, Kennedy grew increasingly disillusioned during his administration with the
quality and character of military advice. The relationship between the president and his military people was, at least on the
surface, entirely correct. Despite some initial strains regarding
the issue of military "muzzling"[21] General Earle Wheeler, chief
of the army under Kennedy, acknowledged that the president
possessed an extraordinary grasp of military issues.[22] For his
part, Kennedy clearly admired the chairman of the Joint Chiefs,
Maxwell Taylor, and the marine commandant, General David
Shoup. Nevertheless, Kennedy confidant Benjamin C. Bradlee
quoted the president as saying, "The first advice I'm going to
give my successor is to watch the generals and avoid feeling
that just because they are military men their opinion on military matters is worth a damn."[23] The president conveyed a
similar sentiment to Norman Cousins in 1963:

> In fact, he [Kennedy] said, some generals believed the
> only solution for any crisis was to start dropping the big
> bombs. When the President would pursue the matter by
> asking how bombing would solve the problem, the replies
> would be far less confident or articulate.[24]

The size of the gulf separating civilian and military officials
on the test ban issue became apparent on June 26, 1963, when
Admiral Anderson, reading a unified Joint Chiefs position paper,
testified before Mississippi Senator John Stennis's subcommittee
in opposition to a comprehensive ban. Why the Joint Chiefs
waited until June to voice their strong reservations is not entirely clear. General LeMay alluded to an answer when he described the Joint Chiefs' reaction to news of the Harriman
mission:

I think we were all caught a little bit by surprise at the
seriousness of the administration trying to get a treaty
signed, up to the point where Mr. Harriman was going
over there. Up until then we hadn't recognized the
seriousness of the approach to this particular treaty.[25]

The question of timing notwithstanding, Anderson enumer-
ated major areas of military concern in the draft comprehensive
treaty under consideration and essentially restated military
skepticism on the inspection issue.[26] Acknowledging that
"different views are held by some of our civilian superiors on
this matter,"[27] including McNamara, Anderson went on to
specify those areas where the Defense Department had
attempted to modify testimony of the Joint Chiefs. The differences between the Joint Chiefs' statement and the Defense
Department's requested revisions illustrates the division between the two groups. For example:

JCS Statement: They conclude, therefore, that the proposed treaty is not consistent with national security, the
Joint Chiefs have expressed their view.

Proposed Change: They conclude, therefore, that the proposed treaty contains certain risks to national security.
These risks the JCS recognize must be balanced against the
risk of losing by continued testing the advantage now held
by the United States in certain areas of nuclear technology,
and the potential deterrent to proliferation which a test
ban might provide.

or:

JCS Statement: Thus, the present military relationship
would be altered in favor of the Soviet Union.

Proposed Change: Thus, the present military relationship
in terms of nuclear warheads capability could be altered
in favor of the Soviet Union as would probably be the case
if both sides continued testing.[28]

It is clear that the military's reservations about the hazards
of a comprehensive ban were not shared by the president or by
other key civilian officials. As ACDA Director Foster testified
before the Stennis subcommittee, "They [Joint Chiefs] are not

making policy decisions which take into account all of the factors that go into this sort of thing, so I do not think it is incumbent upon us to take into account the individual opinions of the Joint Chiefs of Staff."[29] At the same time, military disquiet over the administration's negotiating position was perceived correctly as potentially threatening to the search for political support in Congress. Individual congressmen, both in the Preparedness Investigating Subcommittee and the Foreign Relations Committee, peppered civilian and military officials with questions about military access to the highest decision-making circles. Congressional solicitude for the military's status in the administration was, in fact, so pronounced that the question of whether the Joint Chiefs were adequately consulted became an issue in and of itself. The Stennis subcommittee's chief counsel, James T. Kendall, summed up a fairly strong Senate impression when he defended the subcommittee's solicitation of testimony from military quarters: "I would hope that the fact that the people wore a uniform would not be a factor in your [Franklin Long of the ACDA] thinking that we went to the wrong place."[30]

The administration, most notably Secretary McNamara, went out of its way to reaffirm publicly the central position of the military as an active consultant in the decision-making process. In testimony before the Senate Foreign Relations Committee, the secretary of defense noted, "The Chiefs have met on literally hundreds of occasions in the last two years to consider the proposals that have been under study."[31] His protestations, however, left some senators less than fully convinced. Shortly after McNamara's testimony Senator Barry Goldwater of Arizona asked General LeMay to confirm the secretary's assertion that he had consulted with the Joint Chiefs of Staff. The air force chief of staff responded, "No, he hasn't discussed it with me personally, nor do I remember his discussing it with the Joint Chiefs as a body."[32] In a move designed to defuse criticism of this kind, Joint Chiefs of Staff Chairman Taylor was elevated to full-fledged membership in the Committee of Principals, and Taylor, testifying before the Senate Foreign Relations Committee in defense of the partial test ban accord, acknowledged that

we actively participated in drawing up his [Harriman's] directive. Then during the discussions in Moscow, the

negotiations, all the cable traffic was made available to the
Chairman who made the necessary extracts and reported
daily to the Joint Chiefs of Staff.[33]

It is difficult to challenge the administration's contention
that it included the military in test ban deliberations. The Joint
Chiefs were represented at meetings of the Committee of Principals eight times between July 26, 1962, and July 8, 1963.[34]
In its June 14 meeting, the committee authorized Taylor to
solicit the opinions of the chiefs with regard to a limited ban,
and the chiefs were later involved in preparing the government's directive to the Harriman mission. The chairman, who
did not have a complete treaty in his hands until the conclusion of negotiations, nevertheless had access to all cable traffic
from Moscow. In addition, other members of the Joint Chiefs,
both individually and collectively, met with the president
twice in July to hear Kennedy's case on behalf of the treaty.[35]
Moreover, the Joint Chiefs conducted several conversations
with Secretary Rusk and Ambassador Harriman concerning the
political advantages of the test ban. Even LeMay acknowledged
that the Joint Chiefs "has consulted just about everybody on
the treaty question."[36] The only source of friction, aside from
policy itself, was a feeling among certain members of the Joint
Chiefs that they were being deliberately isolated from
McNamara. General LeMay could not recall any discussions
with the Secretary of Defense in July, and Admiral Anderson,
who officially left his post on August 1, testified:

> to the best of my recollection, Secretary McNamara did
> not discuss this particular treaty with the Joint Chiefs of
> Staff while I was present prior to the first of August. I
> followed the agenda very closely when I was not present.
> I was present at most of the meetings in June and July.
> And while we, the Chiefs, during the latter part of this
> period were discussing our plans to conduct the exami-
> nation of the implications of this particular treaty, to my
> recollection we did not discuss it at that time with Secre-
> tary McNamara.[37]

While there is sufficient evidence to support the contention
that the Joint Chiefs of Staff were consulted on the test ban
matter, it is also clear that the president was attempting to
make it difficult for the military to oppose him. Foremost in

achieving this objective were the unilateral decisions to forestall the resumption of atmospheric testing and to convene the
Moscow talks. LeMay's comment that "we were all caught a
little bit by surprise" is not particularly difficult to understand.
By May 1963 it appeared that the negotiating momentum
generated in the three months following the Cuban crisis had
all but completely evaporated. The inspection issue appeared
no closer to a resolution, and the domestic political mood,
particularly in Congress, was becoming increasingly hostile to
détente. Under these circumstances, it was not unreasonable
for the military to assume that arms control talks would not
lead to an agreement in the near future.

PRESIDENTIAL INITIATIVES

With negotiating positions on both the U.S. and Soviet sides
apparently intractable, the atmosphere in the spring of 1963
was becoming less and less conducive to a major breakthrough.
Under these conditions, the greatest need was for a gesture or
series of gestures that would keep the negotiations alive. Making these gestures went beyond the capabilities of those elements of the executive branch most in favor of achieving an
agreement; witness Dean's and Wiesner's abortive ventures into
personal diplomacy earlier in the year. Instead, they could only
originate in the president—the one institutional figure with the
independent policy-making power and prestige to speak defini-
tively to the Soviets on behalf of the United States.

The need for an initiative that would dispel the mood of
negativism was impressed upon the president by two individuals,
neither of whom occupied an official position in the United
States government. One of these was British Prime Minister
Harold Macmillan, whose determination to break the negotiating logjam was equaled by his apprehension that the failure of
the West to act decisively would doom any possibilities for an
accord. The other was peace activist and *Saturday Review*
editor Norman Cousins, whose unofficial designation as
Kennedy's peace emissary gave him access to Kennedy that
would lead to the historic address at American University in
June.

Macmillan and Kennedy had discussed the question of arms
control as early as December 1961 in Bermuda. At that meeting, the prime minister attempted to convince the president
not to resume atmospheric testing without first taking some

major, concerted initiative to arrest the arms spiral. While
ultimately unable to persuade Kennedy to prevent the resumption of atmospheric testing, Macmillan came away with the impression that

> . . . Kennedy was desperately anxious to postpone the day
> of resuming tests, which he regarded as a confession of
> failure in the diplomatic field. Like me he longed for some
> breakthrough towards peace. My purpose, therefore, was
> to provide him with the necessary ammunition and to
> urge upon him a new effort to deal with the problem as
> a whole.[38]

In March 1963, with the Geneva talks stalemated and the
domestic pressure in the United States making it difficult for
the president to relax the American negotiating position,
Macmillan wrote a letter to Kennedy suggesting, among other
things, the convening of a summit conference with Khrushchev.
Instrumental in the formulation of this initiative was David
Ormsby-Gore, British ambassador to the United States and an
intimate confidant of the president—a fact appreciated by the
prime minister in his own dealings with Kennedy.[39]
Kennedy, while not averse to circumventing his bureaucracy,
was reluctant to engage Khrushchev in high-level summitry,
believing that negotiations were best left to lower diplomatic
levels.[40] In answering Macmillan, Kennedy reiterated his appre-
hensions about summitry and in a follow-up letter added:

> memories . . . of May 1960 are very strong in this country,
> and in my own mind, and I believe that on the historic
> evidence it is not likely that Khrushchev would make
> major changes at a Summit from positions put forward
> under his direction.[41]

Kennedy suggested that as an alternative the Western leaders
propose the convening of a high-level conference, a recommendation that the prime minister ultimately endorsed. Khrushchev's
reply was truculent in tone and highly critical of the Western
insistence on seven inspections, but it did not reject in principle
the dispatching of high-level British and American diplomats
to Moscow. Despite Kennedy's discouragement at the decidedly
hostile tone of Khrushchev's reply, Macmillan persuaded the
president to continue the initiative,[42] and on June 8, the Soviet

premier agreed to convening the conference.

In his June 10 foreign policy address at American University, the president disclosed publicly Khrushchev's acceptance of the joint British-American offer to convene a high-level, tripartite conference in Moscow. He also announced that the United States would not be the first country to resume above-ground nuclear testing. According to Sorensen, those parts of the speech that dealt with nuclear testing were shown to the Joint Chiefs of Staff,[43] but his recollection does not correspond to the testimony of LeMay and Anderson. LeMay recalled, "I did not have any prior knowledge of the suspension of atmospheric testing. I don't think the Joint Chiefs knew about it either."[44] Anderson testified that to "the best of my knowledge the Joint Chiefs, their views were not solicited on the recent suspension of tests in the atmosphere."[45] According to AEC Commissioner Leland Haworth, neither the Joint Chiefs of Staff nor the AEC was consulted in advance of the president's announcement to suspend plans for the resumption of atmospheric testing,[46] and according to Schlesinger's recollections, the speech was not shown to the Joint Chiefs.[47] LeMay acknowledged, however, that Chairman Taylor might have been consulted prior to the president's address.[48]

In retrospect, the greater significance of the president's speech in the long run was his articulation of a concept of détente and in the short run his attempt to convince the Soviets of his real determination to engineer a test ban. While the president had been contemplating a major address on "peace" since the early spring, the advice of Norman Cousins gave his intentions greater immediacy. Cousins had been conveying messages and impressions between the president and Chairman Khrushchev since December 1962. In a conversation with Kennedy in April he noted that hardliners in the Kremlin and the Communist Chinese were putting pressure on the Soviet leader to renounce his "arms control initiative."[49] Clearly, according to Cousins, matters in the Soviet Union were coming to a head. On June 18 Khrushchev was slated to address the Soviet Plenum, and soon after that a major summit conference was scheduled between the Chinese and the Soviets. Without any positive reinforcement from Kennedy and given Khrushchev's post-Cuban missile crisis internal weakness, there was a real danger that the Soviet leader would feel compelled to announce the termination of his "peace" offensive. Cousins recommended that the president deliver a major foreign policy address:

The moment is now at hand for the most important single speech of your Presidency. It should be a speech which, in its breathtaking proposals for genuine peace, in its tone of friendliness for the Soviet people and its understanding of their ordeal during the last war, in its inspired advocacy of the human interest, would create a world ground-swell of support for American leadership.[50]

With the president's concurrence, Sorensen began assembling material for the speech. According to Kennedy's aide:

. . . unlike most foreign policy speeches—none of which was so sweeping in concept and import as this turned out to be—official departmental positions and suggestions were not solicited. . . . He [Kennedy] did not want that new policy diluted by the usual threats of destruction, boasts of nuclear stockpiles and lectures on Soviet treachery.[51]

While Sorensen contended that he and Bundy were the only two presidential advisers who knew of the speech,[52] Adrian Fisher of the ACDA remembered that "like many of the President's speeches, since it was a good speech it's got more authors than you can shake a stick at. Everyone had a finger in it."[53] Schlesinger recalled that while Bundy and Sorensen played the leading roles, he too was involved in drafting the speech.[54] In any event, once Sorensen's initial draft was completed, it was circulated around the executive branch, although not through conventional channels. It was shown to the secretaries of state and defense, and on June 7 Bundy convened a small group including Kaysen, Rostow, Schlesinger, and Sorensen to examine the draft.[55] Llewellyn Thompson remembered that Sorensen read him a draft of the speech over the phone.[56] Finally, at night on June 9 Bundy's deputy Kaysen circulated the speech among cabinet-level departments for "minimum clearance."[57]

FORMULATING A NEGOTIATING POSITION

Once the Soviets' affirmative response to the address became apparent, it became necessary to establish the American negotiating position and to bring it in line with the views of America's Western European allies. Washington's close partner in the test ban initiative was Great Britain. At the end of June,

Kennedy stopped off in London for high-level discussions with Prime Minister Macmillan. Most other NATO members favored a test ban.[58] The Scandinavian countries and Canada saw a test ban as "a step in the direction of reducing tensions in general." The Benelux countries and Italy favored a ban for the same reason but also hoped that an agreement would reduce the prospects of nuclear proliferation, particularly with regard to China and France. Germany was expected to "publicly welcome a test ban agreement." Privately, however, many German leaders worried that a relaxation of tensions might lead to a "softer" American policy toward the Soviet Union. Portugal, Greece, and Turkey supported a test ban in principle. Only France opposed a test ban accord.

A recently declassified ACDA document dated June 20, 1963, and entitled "Points to be Covered in Preparation for the Forthcoming July 15 Mission of Governor Harriman to Moscow" gives some new insight into the administration's negotiating position as it stood on the eve of the Moscow talks.[59] The document divides discussion areas into four main parts:

1. Comprehensive Test Ban Treaty—According to the ACDA, "the initial part of the discussion should deal with a comprehensive test ban treaty." The agency advises the American negotiator to emphasize that the American insistence on seven inspections per year results from the scientific uncertainties regarding the detection of underground tests as distinct from earthquakes. Harriman should make clear that the issue has nothing to do with the political requirements of ratification. The document goes on to suggest that the American negotiator might explore possibilities for breaking the deadlock by dividing inspections into seismic and aseismic zones.

2. Atmospheric, Outer Space, and Underwater Test Ban Treaty With Some Limitations on Underground Tests—On this point the document begins, "The U.S. offer to sign a treaty banning tests in the atmosphere, underwater, and in space remains open. Although the preference is for a comprehensive treaty, if the Soviet Union still cannot be persuaded on the number and role of inspections for underground tests, then a partial treaty may be the best solution obtainable in the present international climate." At the same time, the ACDA notes a basic disadvantage in a partial treaty. Because the Soviet Union lags behind the United States in its knowledge of the effects of underground explosions, it would gain much more from a treaty which allowed unrestricted underground testing. Harriman might, therefore, offer a partial treaty in conjunction with a quota on underground explosions.

3. Relationship of a Test Ban to Nonproliferation of Nuclear Weapons—

The agency document notes, "One of the principal interests of the United States in a test ban agreement is an interest in it as one of a series of steps designed to prevent the proliferation of nuclear weapons throughout the world." Assuming that the Soviets have a similar interest, the document advises Harriman to pursue the point and suggests that the administration might be willing to exert pressure on DeGaulle to gain French compliance. With regard to the MLF, the agency is ambiguous, although it defends the proposal as preventing European states from acquiring their own nuclear capabilities.

4. NATO-Warsaw Nonaggression Pact—The document notes that not enough is yet known about the issue to allow for serious negotiations. Harriman is advised to deflect the issue, although some probing is allowed.

Because Kennedy had such a personal stake in achieving a test ban agreement, the choice of a chief negotiator was especially important. Foy Kohler, the American ambassador to the Soviet Union, might have appeared an obvious choice, but according to Benjamin Read of the State Department, he was treated in effect as *persona non grata* by Khrushchev.[60] Moreover, if Robert Kennedy's views on this matter accurately reflect the president's, then Kohler was certainly not a presidential favorite. Schlesinger quoted Robert Kennedy as follows: "I wasn't too impressed with him [Kohler] at all. He gave me rather the creeps and I don't think he'd be the kind of person who would really get anything done with the Russians."[61] The selection of John McCloy, chairman of the ACDA's General Advisory Committee and a Republican as well, would have helped to deflect partisan attack on Capitol Hill. But McCloy was unavailable for the critical assignment.

In searching for an emissary, the president focused on the Department of State. Mary Milling Lepper, in her analysis of the Test Ban Treaty, reasoned that the State Department was chosen to assuage continuing congressional discomfort over the apparent usurpation of its authority by the ACDA.[62] Moreover, because the ACDA, particularly its director William Foster, had been so vigorous in promotion of a comprehensive ban, the agency had inevitably "stepped on too many toes" in Congress, as Benjamin Read observed.[63]

According to Schlesinger, Rusk suggested the appointment of Averell Harriman as chief negotiator—probably at the suggestion of Carl Kaysen. Kaysen recommended that Rusk's suggestion be acted upon immediately, lest opposition develop in the State Department to Harriman's selection. Harriman was not particularly well liked by State Department regulars, and this probably explains both Kaysen's haste and the subsequent departmental brouhaha over his designation.[64] It is also apparent that Kennedy had had his eye on Harriman at least since April. Cousins reported that upon hearing of Khrushchev's desire to give the negotiations a new impetus, Kennedy retorted, "This looks like a job made to order for Averell Harriman."[65]

The appointment of Harriman was consistent with the president's desire to make the negotiations as much an extension of his own will as politically feasible. The ambassador, with a commitment to arms control equal to that of the president, was nominally a member of the State Department, but in a very real sense not tied to its bureaucratic parochialism. The president, who had employed Harriman's services earlier to resolve the Laos imbroglio, was determined to make the test ban initiative a major test of his personal prestige, and his orchestration of the decision-making process that guided the negotiators was clearly designed to maximize presidential involvement and control. This fact soon became evident to Read and others in the State Department:

> We had suspected it before that time, but it was made explicitly clear in the Moscow discussion, that it was the President's initiative that produced the negotiations. It was not the initiative of the State Department text or anyone else that got this thing going. . . . And the President felt passionately involved in achieving its success.[66]

The selection of the negotiating team and the guidelines for communicating with the delegation were a direct function of the president's desire to control tightly the flow of information between Moscow and Washington. Harriman wanted Kaysen and McNaughton, two early advocates of a limited ban, to accompany him to the negotiations and was insistent on excluding the military from the delegation. Harriman had strong feelings about the need for civilian supremacy over the military, ". . . I'm just trained by experience and knowledge of the need for domination of the military because they are trained to do certain things."[67] At the same time, Kennedy took extraordinary measures to insure the secrecy of deliberations at the White House. After one conversation with the president, Harriman returned to the State Department with specific instructions as to the circulation of cables from Moscow through the executive branch. According to a memorandum on the subject subsequently made available to the Kennedy Library:

1. All substantive communication between Moscow and Washington will be designated BAN, eyes only.
2. Upon receipt in the State Department's Communication Center, incoming messages slugged BAN will be relayed automatically to the White House.
3. The message will then be sent in two copies in sealed envelopes to S/S—Mr. Read. The names of those who see the cables in the Communications Center will be written down.
4. One copy will be put in a brown envelope as a file copy. Another copy for the Secretary of State can be shown by Mr. Read to George Ball and Ambassador Thompson. Test Ban material is to be forwarded to William Foster at the ACDA.[68]

These elaborate security measures demonstrate the extent to which the president attached primary importance to the talks in Moscow. He was especially fearful lest the cables be disseminated to the military, whose reservations about Kennedy's test ban efforts and propensity for leaking might endanger the negotiations. As Read remembered, "This was part of the same feeling of concern on the part of the President that cables that went to the Defense Department would inevitably get into the massive military machinery and the close security that he wanted and insisted on would be jeopardized."[69]

Kennedy himself carefully drew the circle of those involved in drafting the instructions to the Moscow delegation. The original group included the president, Rusk, George Ball, Foster, McNamara, and McCone meeting in the White House Cabinet Room. Included later were U. Alexis Johnson, Edward R. Murrow, Sorensen, and Thompson. But clearly the president "set the tone for outgoing communications."[70] In fact, Read cited one instance in which Kennedy himself drafted a communiqué to Harriman. In a cable to the ambassador following Harriman's first report, Kennedy instructed his negotiator to use the mutual fear of China to wring concessions from Khrushchev:

... I remain convinced, however, the China problem is
more serious than Khrushchev's comments in his first
meeting. I believe you should press the question in a
private meeting with him. I agree that large stockpiles
are characteristic of U.S. and U.S.S.R. only, but consider
the relatively small forces in hands of people like the
Chinese Communists could be very dangerous to all of
us. Further I believe that even the limited test ban can
and should be the means to limit diffusion.[71]

Kennedy can be described in the case of the test ban negotiations as attempting to implement the "China card" strategy in
a way that was to be reversed under Nixon and his successors.
As early as 1960, in a letter from Soviet specialist George
Kennan, the then presidential candidate received the following
advice: "The main target of our diplomacy should be to
heighten the divisive tendencies within the Soviet bloc. The
best means to do this lies in the improvement of our relations
with Moscow."[72]

At best, Kennedy hoped to draw the Soviets into an arrange-
ment that would prevent the proliferation of nuclear weapons
to countries such as China. As early as 1962, in a press conference Kennedy voiced reservations about even an inspected bilateral agreement as long as major nuclear countries remained
unmonitored.[73] For this reason, not only did he and the
ACDA instruct Harriman to pursue the matter of nondiffusion,
but Kennedy also attempted to prod the recalcitrant French
into acceptance of the test ban accord. On July 16 Macmillan
received a letter from Kennedy in which the president suggested offering the French the release of vital nuclear information which until then had been withheld. Kennedy hoped that
in return Paris might be induced to sign the Test Ban Treaty.[74]
The nonproliferation scheme, however, was welcomed with
little enthusiasm either in France or in the Kremlin, and soon
after negotiations began in Moscow, Lord Halisham, leader of
the British delegation, noted that the Americans had virtually
abandoned the idea. This obvious disappointment notwithstanding, Kennedy hoped to exploit the schism over arms control in the Communist camp by appealing to the relative
dovishness of the Kremlin's leaders. By mid-1963 he was fairly
convinced that the Chinese would pose a greater threat to the
United States over the long run, and he told Harriman and

Kaysen upon their leave-taking to Moscow that they could go
as far as they wished "in exploring the possibility of a Soviet-
American understanding with regard to China."[75]

THE MOSCOW NEGOTIATIONS

On July 2 Khrushchev accepted the American offer to negotiate a limited ban, and the tone of the negotiations was set.
Llewellyn Thompson claimed some personal credit for this
about-face on the part of the Soviet leader. According to
Thompson, in a private luncheon conversation Soviet Ambassador Anatoly Dobrynin told him that owing to the prevailing
mood in the Senate, it was impossible for the Kremlin to consider the limited ban as a realistic proposal. Thompson retorted,
"If the President is behind it, the Senate will fall in line."[76]
Thompson surmised that Dobrynin's subsequent report to
Khrushchev resulted in the new Soviet position on a limited
accord.

The negotiations in Moscow progressed despite occasional
vexations over the Soviet desire to conclude a nonaggression
pact in Europe, the American insistence on a written right of
withdrawal, the question of peaceful explosions, and a final
dispute over the extension of the treaty to nonsignatories. It
became clear fairly early that several of Kennedy's objectives
would not be met in Moscow. Almost immediately, Khrushchev
rejected the possibility of making any further concessions on
a comprehensive ban. For his part, Kennedy was not willing to
pay the domestic political price of dropping to fewer than seven
inspections. In addition, Khrushchev refused to discuss the
Chinese issue with Harriman and put off any attempt to negotiate a nonproliferation treaty. At the same time, the Soviets
alternated between pushing for and relaxing on their insistence
to link a partial ban with a wider accord on the European question. Kennedy, who was already concerned about de Gaulle's
refusal to consider a ban on testing and German anxieties on
the same issue, did not want to strain the alliance any further
by negotiating a pact that worried his Western allies. Accordingly, Harriman convinced the Soviets that a nonaggression
pact would require considerable negotiation between the
United States and Western European countries and persuaded
them to detach the issue from test ban questions.

The withdrawal question was less significant in the broad
context of issues dividing the negotiators, but it nevertheless
posed a serious threat to the ultimate conclusion of the treaty.

The Soviets did not want the inclusion of a specific withdrawal clause, because they felt that a written stipulation to that effect would impinge on their unstated sovereign right to withdraw from any treaty once it proved detrimental to the national interest. The Americans, on the other hand, anticipated difficulties with Congress in the absence of a withdrawal clause. The Joint Chiefs, who had powerful friends on Capitol Hill, had made the right of withdrawal a key part of their position. Moreover, Congress feared that were China, a nonsignatory, to develop a significant nuclear capability, it would be incumbent on the United States to resume atmospheric testing—despite the absence of any Soviet violation. Records of cables from Washington to the Moscow delegation indicate that on July 17, Rusk advised Harriman of the importance to Congress of a withdrawal clause.[77] As a consequence, the following compromise wording was incorporated in the treaty: "Each Party shall in exercising its national sovereignty have the right to withdraw from the Treaty if it decides that extraordinary events, related to the subject matter of this Treaty, have jeopardized the supreme interest of its country."[78]

Another troublesome question in which the president took a personal and decisive hand was the issue of peaceful nuclear explosions in the atmosphere. The Soviet draft treaty contained no provision for peaceful explosions. The American draft of August 27, 1962, however, contained a stipulation allowing the detonation of peaceful nuclear explosions in the atmosphere under carefully controlled supervision. This provision was designed to encourage the "Plowshares Program," which was part of the AEC's bureaucratic domain. Kennedy broke the impasse by dropping the American insistence on allowing peaceful nuclear explosions. In return, the Soviets agreed to a less rigorous means for the future revision of the treaty, thus affording the opportunity for amendments allowing peaceful detonations.

At the eleventh hour, a new predicament developed to envelop the British and American allies in their first and only major negotiating dispute. Until then, British-American cooperation had been exceptionally strong. According to Sir Michael Wright, a disarmament expert attached to the British negotiating team in Moscow, the American and British delegations met daily in Moscow to discuss their respective instructions from London and Washington. Wright remembered that there were many different channels of communication between the two

groups "on a low level to a high level."[79] The Soviets proposed
that any country not now a party to the treaty but agreeing to
its provisions in the future should automatically have its name
affixed to the treaty copy kept in each of the original parties'
depositories. The American delegation was apprehensive that
such a procedure might give the Soviets the opportunity to
gain *de jure* American recognition of East Germany by including the Communist government in a treaty to which the United
States was a principal party. Harriman suggested that a stipulation be included in the treaty noting that accession to the agreement by a new government did not imply recognition by
previous signatories. The Soviets, who had made the recognition of East Germany a cornerstone of their policy in Central
Europe, strongly demurred. This impasse was further complicated by Soviet language in the preamble suggesting an
abrogation of the right to employ nuclear weapons, even in
self-defense.

The American insistence on not implying recognition of
new signatories vexed the British. Macmillan wrote in his
diary on July 25, 1963, ironically the day on which the Test
Ban Treaty was initialed:

> . . . The new American clause seemed to go back on the
> compromise already agreed which was quite sensible
> and said that no country *need* accept formal adherence
> from a country with which they were not in relations.
> The other American change was that nothing in the
> Treaty could be taken to prevent the use of nuclear
> weapons in war! This was so absurd as to be hardly
> credible.[80]

According to Schlesinger, Lord Halisham was responsible
for Macmillan's anxiety, an anxiety so pronounced that the
prime minister instructed Gore to intercede personally with
Kennedy. Schlesinger was quite critical of Halisham's part in
the negotiations. He wrote, "Halisham, relying on British
amateur tradition, was ill-prepared in the technicalities of the
problems and was consumed by a desire to get a treaty at almost any cost."[81] Perhaps mindful of Schlesinger's harsh treatment of Halisham, Macmillan wrote in his memoirs some eight
years later, "I can never be sufficiently grateful both to
Halisham and Harriman for the energy and imagination with
which they conducted this delicate negotiation."[82] According

to Schlesinger, Harriman was correct in pressing the issue with the Soviets, and as Harriman later contended, "I am always right when I know I am right. Sometimes I only guess I am right, and then I may be wrong. This time I knew I was right."[83]

Part of the impasse was resolved when the Soviets agreed to shelve any language in the preamble prohibiting the right to use nuclear weapons in wartime. Abram Chayes, the State Department's legal adviser, was particularly insistent on this point, although not for legal reasons. Chayes was convinced that the retention of wording outlawing all nuclear explosions—no matter how ambiguous—would raise serious problems in the Senate, where "the natural tendency would be for opponents of the treaty to try to load on to the reservation as much as they could to attenuate in this way, if not to defeat, the purposes and effects of the treaty."[84] The other outstanding issue was resolved when Fisher and McNaughton engineered a compromise whereby signatories would be required to sign only with governments that they recognized. In the late afternoon of July 25, with Gore and Bundy in the president's office, Kaysen called from Moscow and recommended that Kennedy approve the revised language. The president agreed immediately and phoned Macmillan with the news that the negotiations had been concluded.

With the treaty initialed, Kennedy attempted to tie all loose ends within the executive branch, so that the administration could present a united front in testimony before the Senate. It has already been noted that the Joint Chiefs, apart from Chairman Taylor, were denied direct access to all cable traffic and excluded from active participation in the Moscow negotiations. Once the treaty became a certainty, however, the president and other civilian members of the administration lobbied the Joint Chiefs, both individually and collectively, vigorously and intensively. The main line of argument on behalf of the treaty was that the political value of ratification far exceeded any possible military disadvantages. Nevertheless, the Joint Chiefs calculated that the cost/benefit ratio of treaty ratification could only be met if four conditions were met:

1. The United States should not accept a limitation on testing if the Soviet Union could achieve a major advantage that could not be overcome by the United States under the present treaty.
2. The Test Ban Treaty is acceptable only if clandestine test-

ing by the Soviets would not seriously affect the balance of power.

3. Withdrawal should be uncomplicated, allowing the United States to withdraw upon violation or serious jeopardy to the national interest.

4. If conditions under criteria 1 and 2 are not met, the treaty must convey adequate compensatory advantages elsewhere.[85]

Kennedy, eager to win the support of the Joint Chiefs, offered to attach safeguards to the treaty to meet these conditions. In testifying before the relevant Senate committees, each member of the Joint Chiefs stressed that his endorsement of the treaty was predicated on the enactment of guarantees that the president promised. Even so, there were still some reservations regarding the specific character of these safeguards, as LeMay testified before the Senate Foreign Relations Committee:

> We are all aware of the statement by the President and the Secretary of Defense have made in regard to maintaining a test program and so forth. We have not, however, discussed with them what they mean by that—whether what we consider an adequate safeguard program coincides with their idea on the subject.[86]

EVALUATION

At the outset of this chapter, McGeorge Bundy was quoted as crediting President Kennedy with overcoming the bureaucratic momentum of the arms race through the vigorous exercise of the numerous instrumentalities of presidential power. There is much merit in this argument. Aside from strengthening those elements of the administration most in favor of an arms agreement, Kennedy took independent actions to keep the negotiations alive when they appeared least promising. Gestures such as the Moscow talks initiative, the suspension of atmospheric testing, and the American University address all circumvented routine bureaucratic channels. Once the talks reached the decisive stage, the president sedulously stage-managed the decision-making process and isolated that segment of the executive branch that had proved itself in the past to be least sympathetic to his policy objectives. Indeed, in dealing with the Joint Chiefs of Staff, Kennedy sometimes treated its members as adversaries who had to be confronted after the fact and then pacified with ambiguous concessions. This point was not lost on LeMay, who testified, "I think that the fact that it had been signed had an effect on me. . . . I would think I would have been against it."[87] The impression that the Joint Chiefs were, in fact, forced into endorsing a treaty that they opposed was strong among opponents of the agreement. On September 13 Senator Stennis, who as chairman of the Preparedness Investigating Subcommittee had close ties to the military, charged that the military was coerced into approving the Test Ban.[88] For his part, Kennedy was not so certain that the public support of the Joint Chiefs for the treaty would prevent the military from lobbying behind the scenes to defeat it.[89]

In assessing Kennedy's role, however, one must avoid overestimating the president's capacity to control the flow of events both inside and outside the executive branch. Jacobson and Stein, in distinguishing between the arms control efforts of the Eisenhower and Kennedy administrations, argued that Kennedy's leadership led to the tabling of two treaties in 1962 and conversely Eisenhower's irresolution prevented a nuclear test ban treaty from being tabled earlier.[90] This point is important, and it recognizes the central role of a president in lending coherence to a policy-making system that is centrifugal in character.

At the same time, two points of equal significance must be considered. A limited test ban proposal had been advanced by the Americans and British in 1959, only to be rejected by the Soviets. While it was not packaged in the form of a treaty and while it contained some provision for international inspection, the proposal was not very different in its essence from the draft treaty tabled in 1962. Nevertheless, in July 1963 the Soviets reversed themselves and accepted the partial ban idea. Why they did so is a matter of some question. It is clear that had the president not sustained the test ban initiative, the atmosphere for a Soviet policy switch might not have existed. On the other hand, other factors, peculiar to Soviet politics, might have come into play, such as Soviet economic needs, the rift with China, and the hope that a treaty might prevent the West Germans from acquiring a nuclear capability of their own. Quite possibly the Soviets became aware after the experience of the Cuban missile crisis that they were no match for the United States in terms of nuclear strength. They thus opted for a policy, as represented by the test ban, that would ease tensions and thereby avoid putting them in a position where nuclear inferiority might lead to another political defeat. In this sense, Kennedy's expansion of nuclear forces and willingness to threaten their use over Cuba might have persuaded the Soviets to seek a "breather" in the Cold War. This, parenthetically, was the short-run effect of Kennedy's nuclear policies and his Cuban decision. The long-range impact was to accelerate the development of Soviet nuclear forces. Whatever the motivation, it is impossible to escape the conclusion that Kennedy's successful efforts in signing an accord with the Soviet Union was in no small part a consequence of a major change in Soviet policy.

Closely tied to this point is the fact that the accord finally initialed—while most politically expedient—was not Kennedy's first choice. It is interesting to speculate on what might have occurred had Khrushchev, in his speech of July 2, 1963, agreed to the administration's demand for seven as the minimum number of inspections required for a comprehensive ban. Given the Joint Chiefs' statement of June 26 to the Stennis subcommittee, such an eventuality would most probably have embroiled the president in a public fight with his principal military advisers. As it was, the Joint Chiefs accorded the Nuclear Test Ban Treaty only grudging public support. In a sense, then, Kennedy was fortunate that the Soviets did not force him to fight an internal battle that might have easily resulted in his defeat.

NOTES

1. McGeorge Bundy, "The Presidency and the Peace," *Foreign Affairs* 42 (April 1964): 362-63.
2. Memorandum, W. W. Rostow to McGeorge Bundy and Carl Kaysen, July 5, 1963. John F. Kennedy Library.
3. Benjamin H. Read, recorded interviews by Joseph E. O'Conner and Dennis O'Brien, February 22, 1966, and October 17, 1969, p. 22. John F. Kennedy Library Oral History Program.
4. U.S., Congress, Senate, Committee on Armed Services, Preparedness Investigating Subcommittee, *Hearings: Military Aspects and Implications of Nuclear Test Ban Proposals and Related Matters*, 88th Cong., 1st sess., 1963, p. 156.
5. Samuel P. Huntington, *The Soldier and the State: The Theory and Politics of Civil-Military Relations* (New York: Vintage, 1957), pp. 63-66. See also Bernard Mennis, *American Foreign Policy Officials: Who They Are and What They Believe Regarding International Politics* (Columbus, Ohio: Ohio State University Press, 1971).
6. NSAM No. 55 from President John F. Kennedy to the Joint

Chiefs of Staff on their role in the Cold War. John F. Kennedy Library.

7. *Hearings: Military Aspects . . .* , p. 200.

8. U.S., Congress, Senate, Committee on Foreign Relations, *Hearings: Nuclear Test Ban Treaty*, 88th Cong., 1st sess., 1963, p. 358.

9. See the testimony of Harold Brown, Director of Defense Research and Engineering under Kennedy, in *Hearings: Military Aspects . . .* , pp. 864-65.

10. *Hearings: Military Aspects . . .* , p. 796.

11. *The New York Times*, 1 February 1963, p. 1.

12. *The New York Times*, 12 September 1963, p. 21.

13. *Hearings: Military Aspects . . .* , pp. 305-6.

14. *Hearings: Nuclear Test Ban Treaty*, p. 275.

15. *Hearings: Military Aspects . . .* , p. 303.

16. Marvin Kalb, "What Is Power Doing to the Pentagon," in *Civil-Military Relations and Military Professionalism*, ed. United States Army War College (Carlisle, Pa.: USAWC, 1969), p. 37.

17. Herbert York, recorded interview by Steven Rivkin, June 16, 1964, p. 26, John F. Kennedy Library Oral History Program.

18. *The New York Times*, 21 April 1963, p. 1.

19. *The New York Times*, 5 September 1963, p. 1.

20. *The New York Times*, 5 October 1963, p. 7.

21. U.S., Congress, Senate, Committee on Armed Services, Special Preparedness Subcommittee, *Hearings: Military Cold War Education and Speech Review Policies*, 87th Cong., 1st sess., 1962.

22. Earle Wheeler, recorded interview by Chester Clifton, 1964, p. 5. John F. Kennedy Library Oral History Program.

23. Benjamin C. Bradlee, *Conversations with Kennedy* (New York: Norton, 1975; Pocket Books, 1976), p. 112.

24. Norman Cousins, *The Improbable Triumvirate* (New York: Norton, 1972), p. 135.

25. *Hearings: Nuclear Test Ban Treaty*, p. 382.

26. *Hearings: Military Aspects . . .* , pp. 303-4.

27. Ibid., p. 306.

28. These statements are taken from Anderson's testimony, *Hearings: Military Aspects . . .* , pp. 323-27.

29. Ibid., p. 30.

30. Ibid., p. 147.

31. *Hearings: Nuclear Test Ban Treaty*, p. 111.

32. Ibid., p. 372.

33. Ibid., p. 297.

34. *Hearings: Military Aspects . . .* , p. 608.

35. Ibid., p. 733.

36. Ibid.

37. Ibid., p. 912.

38. Harold Macmillan, *At the End of the Day: 1961-1963*, (New York: Harper and Row, 1973), p. 153.

39. Ibid., p. 469.

40. U.S., President, *Public Papers of the Presidents of the United States* (Washington, D.C.: U.S. Government Printing Office), John F. Kennedy, 1962, p. 136.

41. Macmillan, *At the End of the Day*, p. 465.

42. Macmillan remembers in his diary that "David Gore is confident that the President will agree—if only to please me." Ibid., p. 469.

43. Theodore Sorensen, recorded interview by Carl Kaysen, March 26, 1964, and April 4, 1964, p. 72. John F. Kennedy Library Oral History Program.

44. *Hearings: Military Aspects . . .* , p. 757.

45. Ibid., p. 317.

46. Ibid., p. 297.

47. Personal correspondence, Arthur M. Schlesinger, Jr., to the author, April 23, 1979.

48. *Hearings: Military Aspects . . .* , p. 757.

49. Cousins, *The Improbable Triumvirate*, pp. 114-16.

50. Norman Cousins to the president, April 30, 1963. John F. Kennedy Library.

51. Theodore C. Sorensen, *Kennedy* (New York: Harper and Row, 1965), pp. 730-31.

52. Sorensen interview, p. 72.

53. Adrian Fisher, recorded interview by Frank Sieverts, May 13, 1964, p. 21. John F. Kennedy Library Oral History Program.

54. Schlesinger to author, April 23, 1979.

55. Sorensen interview, p. 72; Arthur H. Schlesinger, Jr., *A Thousand Days* (Boston: Houghton Mifflin, 1965; Fawcett, 1967), p. 822.

56. Llewellyn E. Thompson, recorded interviews by Elizabeth Donahue, March 25, 1964, and Joseph E. O'Conner, April 27, 1966, p. 20. John F. Kennedy Library Oral History Program.

57. Sorensen, *Kennedy*, p. 736. Memorandum, Pierre Salinger to Carl Kaysen, June 9, 1963. John F. Kennedy Library.

58. Memorandum, Thomas L. Hughes to the secretary, "Allied Attitudes on Linking a Test Agreement with a Non-Aggression Pact," July 8, 1963, National Security Files, Box 265, John F. Kennedy Library.

59. "Points to be Covered in Preparation For The Forthcoming July 15 Mission of Governor Harriman to Moscow," June 20, 1963, National Security Files, Box 265, John F. Kennedy Library.

60. Read interview, p. 10.

61. Arthur M. Schlesinger, Jr., *Robert Kennedy and His Times* (Boston: Houghton Mifflin, 1978), p. 501.

62. Mary Milling Lepper, *Foreign Policy Formulation: A Case Study of the Nuclear Test Ban Treaty of 1963* (Columbus, Ohio: Charles E. Merrill, 1971), p. 81.

63. Read interview, p. 11.

64. Ibid., p. 10.

65. Cousins, *The Improbable Triumvirate*, p. 114.

66. Read interview, p. 8.

67. W. Averell Harriman, recorded interviews by Michael Forrestal, April 13, 1964, and Arthur Schlesinger, Jr., January 17, 1965, and June 6, 1965, p. 87. John F. Kennedy Library Oral History Program.

68. State Department Memorandum on Handling BAN. John F. Kennedy Library.

69. Read interview, p. 9.

70. Ibid., p. 3.

71. Ibid., p. 24.

72. George F. Kennan to John F. Kennedy, August 17, 1960. John F. Kennedy Library.

73. *Public Papers . . . Kennedy, 1962*, p. 139.

74. Macmillan, *At the End of the Day*, p. 476.

75. Schlesinger, *A Thousand Days*, p. 825.

76. Thompson interview, p. 9.

77. "Chronological Index and Distribution Sheet on All BAN Messages," National Security Files, Box 265, John F. Kennedy Library.

78. U.S., Department of State, *United States Treaties and Other International Agreements* (Washington, D.C.: Government Printing Office, 1964), p. 1319.

79. Sir Michael Wright, recorded interview by David Nunnerly, May 14, 1969, p. 2. John F. Kennedy Library Oral History Program.

80. Macmillan, *At the End of the Day*, p. 483.

81. Schlesinger, *A Thousand Days*, p. 823.

82. Macmillan, *At the End of the Day*, p. 480.

83. Schlesinger, *A Thousand Days*, p. 830.

84. Memorandum, Abram Chayes to Under Secretary Ball, July 24, 1963, National Security Files, Box 265, John F. Kennedy Library.

85. *Hearings: Military Aspects . . .* , p. 588.

86. *Hearings: Nuclear Test Ban Treaty*, p. 373.

87. Ibid., pp. 371-72.

88. *The New York Times*, 14 September 1963, p. 4.

89. Cousins, *The Improbable Triumvirate*, p. 134.

90. Harold Karan Jacobson and Eric Stein, *Diplomats, Scientists and Politicians: The United States and the Nuclear Test Ban Negotiations* (Ann Arbor, Mich.: The University of Michigan Press, 1966), p. 475.

6.
THE NUCLEAR TEST BAN TREATY AND DOMESTIC POLITICS

At the outset of 1963, there were indications that Kennedy might have serious difficulty in winning congressional support for an arms control agreement. To be sure, the president had emerged from the 1962 Cuban crisis with his public standing appreciably enhanced. George Gallup's American Institute of Public Opinion reported that on October 10, 1961, among respondents to the question: Do you approve or disapprove of the way Kennedy is handling his job as president, 62 percent approved, 22 percent disapproved, and 16 percent offered no opinion. The same survey released on January 20, 1963, found 76 percent approval, 13 percent disapproval and 11 percent no opinion.[1] Nevertheless, Khrushchev's apparent duplicity in stationing offensive missiles so close to American shores along with new questions about Soviet adherence to the agreement that had signaled an end to the crisis led to strong attacks against the administration's attempt to negotiate a treaty that many believed would afford the Soviets a fresh opportunity to engage in strategic treachery. On January 29 shortly after Kennedy announced his decision to postpone underground testing, Republican New York Governor Nelson Rockefeller criticized the administration's alleged intention to engage in "bilateral and secret deals."[2] Later that winter, with the collapse of the New York and Washington talks and with a renewed American effort to achieve a successful negotiating formula, Senator Everett Dirksen of Illinois, the Republican minority leader in the Senate, accused Kennedy of offering too many concessions to the Soviets.[3]

Early in 1963 the potential for partisan division on the test ban issue was strong. The Republican Conference Committee, in a move designed to make a political issue out of the administration's negotiating stance, charged that Kennedy was leading the country into acceptance of a "risky, unenforceable pact" and established a policy-formulating committee, under the chairmanship of a strident test ban opponent, Representative Craig Hosmer of California, to offer a sustained alternative to the administration's "line."[4] In February, Republicans charged that the administration's decision to accept fewer on-site inspections could only jeopardize national security,[5] and in March the Conference Committee revived Latter's "big hole" theory by contending that the test ban pact under consideration would allow for large-scale Soviet cheating.[6] Republican presidential aspirants such as Arizona's conservative Senator Barry Goldwater, sensing political value in the test ban issue, joined their colleagues in attacks on the administration.

The Democratic side was far less united in support of the administration position. While Senator Humphrey took the lead in publicly repudiating Republican charges, other Democrats were no less vocal in expressing their reservations about a comprehensive ban. On February 21 Connecticut Senator Thomas Dodd, leveling a strong blast, accused the administration of offering too many concessions to the Soviets.[7] Moreover, two respected defense-oriented members of the Democratic party, Senators Henry Jackson of Washington and Stuart Symington of Missouri, questioned the administration's alleged tendency to lower inspection requirements in return for negligible Soviet concessions.[8]

THE "TEST BAN CAMPAIGN"

The growing possibility of a concerted Republican campaign to defeat any comprehensive treaty and the uncertainty regarding the degree of Democratic support potentially available in the Senate forced the administration to devote more attention to the cultivation of support in the domestic political arena. In January 1962 Sorensen sent Kennedy a memo contending that most of the public opposed a resumption of nuclear testing.[9] By January 1963, however, Kennedy's political operatives became concerned that the administration's possible misperception of public attitudes had led it into complacency regarding the exigencies of domestic political mobilization. According to political adviser Fred Dutton, the vigorous activities of pro-ban groups in the United States did not necessarily reflect widespread, grass-roots support for the administration's bargaining position: "Most people outside of the ban-the-bomb groups are poorly informed and increasingly suspicious on the subject."[10]

Public opinion studies conducted at the time tended to endorse Dutton's concern. A study published in the *Public Opinion Quarterly* during the summer of 1963 indicated the existence of two fundamental groups among the public.[11] Pro-ban advocates tended to come from the better-educated stratum of society; those opposed, with some exceptions, were among the less educated. The study also found that those with less education were at the same time less fearful of nuclear fallout. They were also opposed to granting the Soviets the right to conduct tests while simultaneously supportive of the American right to do so. Those with more education were considerably more anxious about nuclear war, and they challenged the right of either superpower to conduct nuclear tests.

With a renewed emphasis on winning support outside the executive branch, the administration focused its attention on two areas. On one hand, an attempt was made to establish better communications between the administration and Democratic senators publicly opposed to or undecided about the merits of a comprehensive ban. AEC Commissioner Haworth engaged in extensive conversations with the chairman of the Joint Committee on Atomic Energy, John O. Pastore of Rhode Island, and Adrian Fisher did the same with Senator Albert Gore of Tennessee. According to Mary Milling Lepper, these contacts impressed on the administration the existence of limited support for a comprehensive ban and significant support for the negotiation of a partial treaty.[12] On the other hand, the administration sought to rebut opposition arguments that pro-ban advocates believed were receiving undue media attention.[13] In response to Senator Dodd's attack on the administration's test ban policy, Fisher wrote a letter to *The Washington Post*, arguing that militarily there was more benefit than disadvantage in a comprehensive pact.[14] Moreover, favorably inclined senators were enlisted in the effort to build support for a test ban. In addition to Humphrey's spirited public attacks against the administration's opponents, Senator Pastore collaborated in arranging testimony before the Joint Committee on Atomic Energy to give administration members a full public hearing.

The centerpiece of the administration's public lobbying efforts was the president himself. In a news conference on February 22, 1963, Kennedy explained the administration's rationale in seeking to curb the arms race, "Well, in my judgment, the major argument for the test ban treaty is the limiting effect it might have on proliferation."[15] On March 21 the president reaffirmed his commitment to achieve a test ban accord by stating that despite the existence of considerable opposition to his policy of negotiation with the Soviets, he would continue to press for an agreement.[16] In May the president lent urgency to the achievement of a test ban agreement by reiterating his belief that failure to reach an accord in the near future would lead to widespread proliferation of nuclear weapons. Clearly Kennedy was staking his own prestige on the success of arms control negotiations.

The president's involvement in marshaling support outside the executive branch for his administration's test ban position was an extension of his view of the president's role in mobilizing public opinion. As Sorensen noted:

> . . . no problem of the Presidency concerned him more than that of public communication—educating, persuading and mobilizing that opinion through continued use of the political machinery, continued traveling and speaking and above all, a continued attention to the mass media: radio, television, and the press.[17]

At the same time, the president understood that the specific issue of arms control required special sensitivity to the inherent, anti-Communist sentiment of the American people. The president had to accentuate the pitfalls in failure to negotiate a treaty without appearing too soft on the issue of communism and the Soviet Union. The latter perception was already gaining adherents among right-wing segments of the population. Addressing himself to this charge, Kennedy was careful to associate himself with ultraconservative concerns while at the same time pointing to the inherent peril in a position that took no cognizance of strategic realities. In a press conference dated February 14, 1962, the president responded to a question regarding the alleged "no win" policy of his administration:

> Of course, every American . . . wants the United States to be secure and at peace and they want the cause of freedom

around the world to prevail. . . . We want to do that, of course, without having a nuclear war. Now if someone thinks we should have a nuclear war in order to win, I can inform them that there will not be a winner in the next nuclear war, if there is one.[18]

Kennedy was not the first president to seek a balance between the objectives of anticommunism and nuclear war avoidance, but he was the most clear-cut up to that time in articulating publicly this complementarity as the governing ideology of American foreign policy in the postwar era. In large part, Kennedy articulated this position because he believed it. At the same time, the need to make frequent references to this duality was in no small measure a consequence of political exigencies. Kennedy recognized that his entire policy of détente, including the centerpiece—arms control—could only survive the wear and tear of the policy-making process if it could be framed in terms of protection from the two greatest threats to the national interest: communism and nuclear war. He recognized that given the strong impulse within the public and Congress to attach greater priority to the anti-Communist tendency, only the prestige of the presidency could possibly legitimize accommodationist policies as consistent with the national interest. George Kennan confirmed this analysis in an interview conducted by the Kennedy Library:

He [Kennedy] was very troubled about this problem [negotiations with the Soviet Union] because, having been in Congress, he was very sensitive to the strong anti-Communist feelings that were prevalent in a portion of the electorate and in a large portion of Congress. He wanted to handle this problem in such a way as to make progress in composing our differences . . . , but not to get himself attacked at home for being soft on Communism or anything of that sort.[19]

In a sense, Kennedy was better equipped to achieve this balance in 1963 than he was in the earlier years of his presidency. By appearing to act decisively and courageously in facing down Khrushchev over Cuba, the president was able to dispel any notion that his was, as right-wing critics charged, an administration of surrender. According to Sorensen, 1963 was not a year marked by radical departures in American foreign policy; the president had extended the "olive branch" earlier.[20] Instead, it was a year in which political circumstances changed to allow the president to challenge the strong anti-Communist tendencies in the electorate and in Congress. This new flexibility Sorensen cited as a major consequence of the Cuban missile crisis.

It is clear that Kennedy gave extraordinary attention to developing a climate of opinion that would sustain his test ban initiative and the treaty initialed in Moscow on July 25. It is also clear that the test ban was the centerpiece of a policy of détente that would ultimately—or so it was hoped—be linked to other areas of Soviet-American relations.[21] The vigorous application of presidential power outside the executive branch was a consequence of several factors. First, Kennedy himself viewed the presidency as the leading institutional source of political opinion in the United States. Second, the president, along with other members of the administration, saw Congress as the most serious potential threat to his policy of détente. Kennedy assumed that by creating a domestic mood of receptivity to greater flexibility in Soviet-American relations, he would be able to apply pressure on Congress to support him. Third, Kennedy understood that only a president could legitimize policies that appeared to be innovative within the framework of the foreign policy consensus that had guided the United States since the end of World War II. Fourth, the president was determined not to repeat the mistakes that Woodrow Wilson had made in his League of Nations fight. In an interview conducted by Robert Stein, editor of *Redbook* magazine, on August 1, 1963, Kennedy argued that Wilson's failure to mobilize public support in his own behalf had spelled disaster for the League initiative.[22] A dialogue between the president and members of the Citizens Committee for a Nuclear Test Ban on August 7, 1963, shows that Kennedy was extremely conscious of the Wilson debacle. Paraphrasing Kennedy, Cousins reported, "Ever since Woodrow Wilson, a President had to be cautious about bringing a treaty before the Senate unless he had a fairly good idea where the votes would come from."[23]

Kennedy believed that the expansion of public interest beyond select interest groups would eventually work to his advantage. No doubt, he was aware of the institutional singularity of the presidency as reference point for the largest possible national constituency. He assumed that with an enlarged scope of public involvement, the tendency of the public to support rather than oppose him would provide his efforts with an incalculable political asset. Kennedy reflected on this need in his interview with Stein:

A great mass of people are frequently not heard or may
not be informed, may not understand the argument,
may feel the arguments are too complicated, may be too
involved in their own private lives that they don't have
time to take an informal interest in world events or in
great national issues. Therefore, the field is left to a few
participants on both sides. I think that the wider we can
spread this debate the better off we will be.[24]

Kennedy's personal approach to the problem of public
mobilization on the test ban issue and the collateral issue of
détente was essentially twofold. First, the president made clear
in numerous public speeches, interviews with the print media,
and television and radio addresses that the administration's
commitment to the Test Ban Treaty was derivative of a strongly felt presidential initiative. In some respects, the substance
of his message was less important than the added measure of
credibility invested in the administration's position by its
identification with the presidential office.

Another, more subtle approach to the problem of public
mobilization was the president's collaboration with the pro-ban
lobby, the Citizens Committee for a Nuclear Test Ban, headed
by Norman Cousins and Ambassador James J. Wadsworth.
The number of groups favoring a test ban was far greater than
the number opposed—an interesting situation considering that
in the late 1970s, the situation would reverse itself. Those
groups that were most involved in the test ban debate were
generally in Kennedy's favor. The forces that opposed the
treaty were few and invariably not well organized. One notable
exception was the National Committee Against a Test Ban,
formed by six editors of the conservative periodical, *The National Review*. Pro-ban advocates, on the other hand, were well
organized even before the debate over the Test Ban Treaty.
During the 1961 congressional debate over the establishment
of the ACDA, no fewer than thirteen disarmament groups
testified in favor of the agency. These groups were ultimately
to serve as a natural constituency for the ACDA.

Pro-ban forces had injected themselves into the test ban
controversy well before the treaty was initialed on July 25.
Earlier that year, groups such as the Dentists Committee for a
Sane Nuclear Policy, the California Young Democrats, the
Women's Strike for Peace, along with groups of church leaders,
business executives, scientists, and academicians had at one

time or another taken public action in support of negotiations. On the eve of Harriman's departure to Moscow, in a carefully orchestrated media event, the ambassador was handed a petition with 30,000 signatures. Wadsworth, who in April had chided Hosmer for presuming to speak for all Republicans, had simultaneously urged Kennedy to educate the public to the hazards of nuclear testing.[25] In July he promised to support the treaty but reserved the right to differ with Kennedy on matters of political strategy.[26]

With the signing of the Test Ban Treaty, however, the president was interested in harnessing the resources of these groups toward a more coordinated lobbying effort. The newly reconstituted Citizens Committee met with the president on August 7 in the White House. The group apprised the president of its organizational framework and the extent of its support. Kennedy, in turn, offered his services to the committee and then suggested areas where it might focus its activities.[27] Over the next month and a half, the president so closely monitored the efforts of the committee that he personally targeted senators such as Henry Jackson for special interest group attention and approved newspaper and television advertisements. The president also directed the committee to concentrate its efforts on swing states such Colorado, Illinois, Iowa, Missouri, Ohio, South Dakota, and Washington.[28]

With Kennedy so convinced that a major effort to reach public opinion was necessary for ratification of the Test Ban Treaty, a major question presents itself: To what extent did the president's efforts lead to the overwhelming success of his battle to win the endorsement of the Senate? It is clear that some change occurred, both in public and congressional attitudes, between the advent of the Harriman mission and the date on which the Senate ratified the treaty. Kennedy, for example, doubted on August 7 that a vote taken that day would produce the necessary two-thirds Senate majority.[29] Moreover, influential senators such as Jackson and Dirksen did not commit themselves in favor of the treaty until September.

Public attitudes were even more subject to change. According to Cousins, private polls conducted shortly after the successful negotiations in Moscow indicated that while the opinion trend was moving away from support for nuclear testing, congressmen were receiving mail showing a proportion of ten to one and in some cases twenty to one against the Test Ban Treaty. In the White House meeting of August 7 a tally by congres-

sional liaison Larry O'Brien came up with a ratio of fifteen to
one against the treaty in letters to Congress. A check of White
House mail found that while the test ban issue evinced relatively little interest, the number of letters opposing the ban
exceeded those in favor by a large margin.[30] But by August 27
the tide began to turn, with pro-ban letters trailing anti-ban
letters by a margin of three to two. By September letters in
favor of the treaty took a decisive lead.

The extent to which letters accurately reflect public opinion
is indeed open to question. Robert Dahl, in his study of Congress and foreign policy, noted that "mail may not be representative, and the Congressman may not be guided by it. He
may look upon it as largely the work of chronic letter-writers
and cranks. Or he may suspect that the avalanche has been
carefully engineered."[31] In the case of the Nuclear Test Ban
Treaty, there was a strong feeling among administration supporters that the mail against ratification could be traced to a
concerted campaign. Senator George Aiken of Vermont noted
on September 18 that most of the mail came from Texas and
California, where right-wing groups tended to be most prominent.[32] Kennedy himself had a rather jaundiced view of letter
writers. According to Schlesinger, in the week following
Kennedy's delivery of the American University address, there
were 896 letters sent to the White House, 861 in favor and 25
against. In contrast, that same week the freight rate bill generated 25, 232 letters. According to Schlesinger, the president
was not incredulous. "That is why I tell people in Congress that
they're crazy if they take their mail seriously."[33]

While changes in the ratio of letters for and against the treaty
may not be indicative of the movement of public opinion
during this period, public opinion polls are available to corrobo-
rate the conclusion that change did in fact occur. A Harris Poll
conducted in the early part of July disclosed:[34]

Unqualified approval for negotiations	47%
Qualified approval	20
Opposed	17
Not sure	10

On September 1, 1963, more than a month after the initialing
of the Moscow treaty, the Harris Poll indicated the existence
of an appreciable rise in support:[35]

Approved	81%
Opposed	8
Qualified approval	11

In assessing Kennedy's role in mobilizing the public to support his test ban initiative, it is important to consider those conditions that invest public opinion with any significance. Taken alone, public opinion is essentially inert. The public as a whole, excluding individual interest groups, is neither sufficiently organized nor interested to act politically on its foreign policy attitudes. Even as voters, members of the public rarely choose candidates according to their foreign policy preferences. Part of the explanation is the relative unimportance to the public of foreign policy issues compared with domestic issues. Another reason is the general convergence of foreign policy platforms of the two major parties, which make it difficult for the voter to discern significant foreign policy differences at election time.

Nevertheless, in a competitive electoral system, there is a natural tendency for parties to divide where partisanship offers some promise of significant political reward. At times the basis for partisan division can involve a matter of conscience or substance. For example, Eisenhower admonished Kennedy privately that while he could support virtually all the new president's foreign policy initiatives, in the event Kennedy changed the government's China policy, he would be forced to reenter public life.[36] At other times, partisanship might emerge on a foreign policy issue, not because the party in opposition is substantially in disagreement with the administration, but rather because it senses that by making an issue of the president's handling of a specific situation, it can weaken his public esteem and hence reduce his political standing. For example, after the Cuban missile crisis, the president's initially high standing in public opinion polls was progressively eroded by a barrage of Republican attacks charging him with ignoring postcrisis Soviet subterfuge in Cuba. A Gallup Survey covering the period February 24 to May 24, 1963, asking respondents if they approved or disapproved of Kennedy's handling of the Cuban situation, demonstrated a significant and steady drop-off in support among Republicans, Democrats, and Independents.[37] Once Republicans saw an initial payoff in attacking the administration, they escalated their criticisms to produce further erosion in the president's position. Public opinion is thus relevant in indicating those areas that can be exploited for partisan gain.

Aside from the relationship between partisanship and public opinion polls, congressional voting patterns are often a function of popular attitudes—sometimes regional—that have little direct bearing on foreign policy. While presidents can often command support on foreign policy matters that is not forthcoming on domestic issues, it is not always possible to compartmentalize presidential performance in these two areas. A drop-off in support on the domestic issue of highly intense concern can make it easier for or even compel legislators to withdraw their support on foreign policy issues and vice versa.

In the case of the Test Ban Treaty, the civil rights issue illustrates this phenomenon. Even as the test ban issue was developing steam in 1963, the unfolding civil rights drama managed to capture greater popular attention. According to Sorensen, Kennedy's American University address was overshadowed by the president's civil rights message delivered the next day.[38] The greatest source of popular concern was in the South, where the civil rights movement was concentrating most of its activity. As a consequence of his strong public stand in favor of civil rights, the president was experiencing noticeable slippage in the polls. A Harris Poll, quoted in *Newsweek* on July 8, 1963, noted that the president's general popularity had fallen five points between May and July.[39] Whereas nationally support for his civil rights program garnered 49 percent approval, in the South only 25 percent offered their support, reflecting regional distinctions regarding the president's popularity in general. In the Northeast, the president's popularity stood at 65 percent and in the West and Midwest at 64 percent. In the South, the president was supported by only 49 percent of those who responded. The Gallup Poll found even greater slippage in the South. Whereas the president's popularity in the South stood at 52 percent in late May, it fell to 33 percent in June as a consequence of his civil rights speech.[40] In July and September, Kennedy's public standing in the South rose to 44 percent, but in October, following the convulsions in Birmingham, it declined to 40 percent. The fact that his popularity was slipping was not lost on the president, who acknowledged to black leaders shortly before embarking on his triumphant European tour that the civil rights issue was creating serious difficulties for his presidency.

It is not surprising, then, that among the nineteen votes opposing final ratification of the Test Ban Treaty, the largest single bloc, nine senators, was composed of Southern Democrats. Naturally, Southern senators tended to reflect the general conservatism of the region with regard to national security matters, but at the same time, many Democrats and Republicans who were just as hard-line on the question of Soviet-American relations voted in support of the treaty. It is possible that the unpopularity of the president in the South allowed those opposing legislators to vote against the president or compelled them to vote against Kennedy on this issue lest their support be construed as endorsement of his civil rights policy.

The failure of the Republicans, on the other hand, to mount a serious challenge against the Test Ban Treaty can also be related to the climate of public opinion. To be sure, as *New York Times* columnist Max Frankel noted on the day before the treaty was initialed in Moscow, the president's extreme secrecy and the limited nature of the pact made it difficult for his senatorial critics to challenge him.[41] Republicans had been warning in and out of Congress that a comprehensive treaty would jeopardize national security; presented with a treaty that met these objections, Republican lawmakers were hard-pressed to challenge the president.

At the same time, it was clear to many Republicans that the Test Ban Treaty was not an issue that could generate a significant amount of political capital in opposition. This reality was supported by a Harris Survey published on August 26, 1963, which demonstrated that while the president could be beaten in 1964 on economic and civil rights issues, 81 percent of the public supported him on his handling of Khrushchev.[42] Coming, with some exceptions, from areas where the president's popularity was still over 50 percent, Republican legislators such as George Aiken and Pennsylvania Senator High Scott and former Presidents Herbert Hoover and Dwight Eisenhower tendered immediate support. While presidential aspirants such as Richard Nixon and Nelson Rockefeller attacked the "military and political assumptions" that underlay the treaty,[43] even they supported ultimate ratification. Clearly as one Republican senator told *Newsweek* on August 5, "I don't see any political mileage in opposing the treaty. It is very likely that the Senate would approve such a treaty."[44]

SENATE ENDORSEMENT

The absence of any substantial political value in opposing the Test Ban Treaty helped to forge the bipartisan consensus that ultimately produced such an enormous victory for Kennedy in the Senate. The president, however, with an eye to 1964 and commitment to achieving as near a unanimous vote as possible, did not take Republican or Democratic support for granted. Sensitive to Wilson's cataclysmic personal and national defeat some forty-five years earlier and convinced that his Democratic predecessor had needlessly alienated the Senate, Kennedy made certain to apprise key senators and Senate committees on developments from Moscow. Montana Senator Mike Mansfield, then Democratic majority leader of the Senate, recalled that a tentative test ban agreement was forwarded to the Foreign Relations Committee two weeks before its initialing in Moscow.[45] In addition, the president dispatched Secretary Rusk and ACDA Director Foster to speak individually with every senator while test ban talks were in progress.[46] On July 24, Secretary Rusk briefed members of the Senate Armed Services Committee and the Joint Committee on Atomic Energy, two committees that had been particularly inclined to criticize the administration's previous negotiating position. From these conversations, it became clear to the administration that the treaty would have difficulty passing the Senate if attached to a non-aggression pact.[47]

Spurred by the president's stated desire to achieve "quick action" on ratification, Senate leaders of the Democratic party mobilized their legislative forces. At times their attempt to build broad, bipartisan support backfired as, for example, in the case of Humphrey's proposal to send a bipartisan congressional delegation to Moscow for the official signing ceremony. Republican leaders such as Bourke Hickenlooper of Iowa and George Aiken of Vermont feared that by going to Moscow, they would commit themselves to voting for the treaty even before Senate hearings convened. Arkansas Democrat J. William Fulbright, chairman of the Foreign Relations Committee, also opposed the idea on the grounds that it would create an issue that would deflect attention from the treaty itself. Ultimately this wrangle was resolved with Republicans Aiken and Leverett Saltonstall, from Kennedy's home state of Massachusetts, accompanying the delegation.

With senators gradually declaring their intentions with regard to the treaty, Kennedy administered the decisive gesture

in mid-September. On July 28 Senator Dirksen, the Republican
minority leader, had objected to the treaty on the grounds
that it rested too heavily on Soviet good faith. In a meeting
with Dirksen on September 9 the president assured the Republican leader of certain guarantees that would safeguard the
security of the United States. These guarantees, contained in a
public letter to Dirksen and Mansfield dated September 11,
included commitments to continue an underground testing
program, to maintain preparedness for possible resumption of
testing in prohibited environments, and to continue research
in the detection of underground tests, and a stipulation that
the president still retained the right to employ nuclear weapons
for self-defense purposes.[48]

These provisions were designed to satisfy the reservations
voiced by the Joint Chiefs in their testimony before the Preparedness Subcommittee and the Foreign Relations Committee. In a larger sense, however, the commitment to maintain
vigilance in the face of continued Soviet hostility was designed
to put the treaty in its proper perspective. Kennedy was
essentially assuring the public, Congress, and the Joint Chiefs
of Staff that by engaging in a nuclear test ban treaty, the administration was merely committing itself to a course of action
that had in the past enjoyed widespread and bipartisan support,
that is, the balancing of the goals of nuclear war avoidance and
anticommunism. Dirksen, in supporting the treaty unreservedly,
clearly associated the Republican party with the goals of the
Democratic president. Items Dirksen listed in favor of the treaty
included reference to the fact that the Republican party platform of 1960 had pledged to seek an early agreement to forego
nuclear tests in the atmosphere.[49] In this regard, Kennedy's
policy was correctly seen as a culmination of efforts begun by
his Republican predecessor.

ASSESSMENT

At the beginning of 1963, opposition to the test ban was
strong. Moreover, public opinion polls, newspaper editorials,
and letters to Congress at the inception of the treaty debate
did not show strong support for the president's initiative. Clearly, the intense lobbying efforts of interest groups in favor of
the treaty and the president's own orchestration of domestic
public opinion had an impact in making the political climate
more favorable.

At the same time the Test Ban Treaty must be considered

in its proper perspective. The treaty that was ultimately
adopted and presented to the Senate for ratification was a
far cry from the comprehensive pact that had mobilized such
intense criticism earlier in the year from Republicans and
Democrats alike. Indeed, the treaty that ultimately evolved
was closer to the original thinking of Senate Democrats such
as Dodd, Pastore, and Gore than to the more ambitious goals
originally favored by the president. One can make a strong
argument for the case, as Max Frankel did in 1963, that the
treaty passed so overwhelmingly because, indeed, it was so
innocuous.

This does not mean that there were not serious objections
to the treaty as it was subsequently presented to the Senate.
From within the administration, the Joint Chiefs clearly had
strong reservations about its effect on the country's military
posture. Defense-minded Democrats such as Henry Jackson
and other members of the Preparedness Subcommittee endorsed the treaty with great reservations. Irreconcilable anti-
Communists such as Strom Thurmond of South Carolina were
opposed to any treaty that promised some thaw in Soviet-
American relations.

Kennedy's ability to circumvent this resistance is testimony
not only to his personal political capabilities but to the institutional role of the presidency as it relates to public opinion,
Congress, and partisan conflict. It is clear that no other figure
in the American political system can command the same attention for his point of view as a president. Presidents enjoy a
virtual monopoly on the flow to the public of information
pertaining to national security and foreign policy in general.
As a consequence, those who oppose the president's point
of view are often hard-pressed to find a constituency that can
serve as a political base for effective criticism. Translated into
the hard currency of political support and opposition, this
asymmetry between the wide scope of presidential reach and
the relatively narrow domain of his opposition results in an
impressive asset to presidential power.

There are, of course, exceptions to this rule. Interest groups,
when they are able to mobilize intense support from a specific
segment of the population, can periodically challenge or at
least neutralize presidential power. Congress can occasionally
frustrate presidents if the issue under consideration touches
on its constitutional prerogatives, such as the ability to control
appropriations. The weakness of interest groups is that they are
most powerful on issues that concern only small portions of

the population. On symmetrical issues, such as arms control, they must contend with the president's ability to reach a larger constituency. The fragmentation of authority and power within each house of Congress makes it relatively simple for the legislators to attack presidents but almost impossible for them to offer creditable alternative courses of action.

The only institution capable of challenging the president's political reach is the opposition party. The opposition party has a large public base of support from which it draws a natural constituency. Moreover, because its leaders are often perceived by the public and particularly by the media as part of a counterelite, the party out of power is often called upon to offer opposing assessments to those of the president. For example, newspaper reports of Kennedy's American University address were balanced by the exposure of Republican charges that the address represented a "soft line" and attacks by Goldwater and Dirksen as to the utility of the Moscow confer- ence.[50] Even though in these cases the president is still at an advantage, he will nevertheless usually attempt to frame his policies in a way that will prevent the surfacing of partisan dif- ferences. For example, during the 1962 campaign Kennedy was careful to accentuate that neither he nor Eisenhower had "attempted to make any partisan issue out of foreign policy."[51] This deference to Eisenhower and fear of the possible conse- quences of partisan division was also evident in Kennedy's China policy. Following the initialing of the Test Ban Treaty, Kennedy went out of his way to build a bipartisan support in Congress and had CIA Director John McCone brief Republican presidential aspirant Nelson Rockefeller.[52] Clearly the threat of partisan opposition was one that Kennedy took seriously.

Kennedy's success in the test ban issue was as much a result of the absence of a strong, organized opposition as it was a con- sequence of his mobilization efforts. Interest groups opposed to the treaty were few and badly organized. Congress, particu- larly the Senate, was split by committee and region. The Repub- lican party, seeing no political payoff in opposition and itself linked to the treaty through Eisenhower, jumped on the band- wagon fairly early. The coalition that ultimately opposed Kennedy, made up principally of Southern Democrats, had little constituency support outside their region.

Kennedy, who fashioned himself a mobilizer, believed that government policy derived its legitimacy from the support of the people. Accordingly, the president's role was to educate and persuade, to build a constituency behind articulated policy.

In essence, though, despite Kennedy's assiduous cultivation of public opinion in 1963, a major portion of his success was attributable to the largely self-legitimizing character of government policy. Public attitudes on foreign policy questions often change to accommodate administration reversals, providing, of course, that there is no strong, organized opposition to challenge the change. The same may be said of the Nuclear Test Ban Treaty. Once the treaty was signed, no doubt many people assumed that the United States had already committed itself to a course of action. Once this occurs, and as long as the president manages to defuse substantial partisan opposition, public support—which is generally fluid in areas where public awareness is relatively low—will eventually be forthcoming.

The role of the president in this case is to associate himself and his office with a specific policy. In doing so, the president does more than persuade. Instead, he invests his administration's policy with the official stamp of legitimacy that only a president can provide. Because people generally look to the president as their source of information and interpretation of the outside world, his strong identification with government policy is usually converted into public support.

In a sense, a similar analysis may be applied to Congress. Congress's influence in foreign policy even today is primarily, according to James A. Robinson, "to legitimate and/or to amend recommendations initiated by the executive to deal with situations usually identified by the executive."[53] With regard to treaty matters, the power of endorsement is usually translated into acceptance of presidential initiatives. Cecil Crabb noted that between 1789 and 1963, the Senate approved without change 69 percent of those treaties presented to it by the president. Of the remaining 31 percent, modifications were made in 18 percent.[54] According to Aaron Wildavsky's figures, between 1948 and 1964, Congress accepted only 40.2 percent of the president's domestic policy initiatives. During the same period of time, it rejected only 26.7 percent of the president's defense policy measures and only 29.3 percent of those policies relating to treaties, general foreign relations, and foreign aid.[55] According to Wildavsky, in the realm of foreign policy there had not been a single major issue on which presidents, when they were serious and determined, failed.[56] In the 1970s, the trend reversed itself somewhat. In the early 1970s, Congress passed constraining legislation such as the War Powers Act. In the mid-1970s, Congress prevented Presidents Ford and Carter from intervening in the Angolan Civil War and bailing out the Thieu regime in South Vietnam. In the late 1970s, the Senate even managed to deny passage of the SALT II agreement. Nevertheless, it remains to be seen whether these measures are part of a long-term trend, either constitutionally or politically. Given a resurgence of Cold War thinking in the United States and the recrystallization of opinion around a crisis mentality, the 1980s might again witness a period of presidential predominance in foreign policy.

Among the many powers available to presidents in the realm of foreign policy, perhaps none is as potent as their capacity to create irreversible, de facto situations by undertaking independent initiatives. In the case of the Nuclear Test Ban Treaty, once the president authorized the initialing of the treaty in Moscow, it became a fact that its opponents could not easily reverse. Harry Byrd, a strong antitreaty senator from Virginia, noted this point in discussions before the Preparedness Subcommittee:

> I have a feeling that the buildup of propaganda or whatever one might wish to term it in support of this treaty has amounted to an overkill, and I feel that if we reject this treaty—and I have not yet made up my mind whether I am going to vote for or against it—but one of the factors which is disturbing me tremendously . . . is the one concerning overkill in the sense that I have just referred to it. I am afraid that if we now reject it, after all of the buildup that we have witnessed, the impact upon other countries and our relations with other countries is going to be terrific.[57]

This is not to say that Kennedy, in the case of the Nuclear Test Ban Treaty, operated free from constraint. On the contrary, the strength of his performance in 1963 lay in his ability to gauge the extent to which the domestic political system would bend to conform to his policies. In 1963, with national elections pending, the Republican party was primed to make national security an issue, just as Kennedy did in his successful pursuit of the presidency three years earlier.[58] Accordingly, Kennedy had to insure that a fruitful policy of arms control did not appear to favor the objective of nuclear war avoidance over containment of the Communist threat.

Kennedy's approach was, therefore, persistent yet simultane-

ously cautious. He wanted a comprehensive ban but in response
to his reading of domestic pressures refused to move beyond
the minimum of seven annual inspections. It has already been
noted that respected members of the administration such as
Robert McNamara and Jerome Wiesner were willing to accept
six and five inspections respectively, and Macmillan backed
their position. But Kennedy calculated that given the existing
climate of opinion in the public and Congress, seven would
have to be the minimum number. As Sir William Penney,
a scientific expert attached to the British delegation to Moscow,
told Macmillan, ". . . it's not science but politics which holds
back the President."[59]

In public speeches and in written commitments to Congress,
Kennedy reiterated that the Soviets had not changed their
character appreciably and that the United States still put a
premium on military readiness. Whether this assertion would
have carried a negotiated comprehensive pact, even with a provision for seven inspections, is questionable. It is clear, though,
that the treaty finally signed was in itself tame enough and consistent enough with policies previously endorsed by the Republican party to insure significant bipartisan support. The Test
Ban Treaty did represent an incremental break from the past.
Moreover, it represented an opportunity for public and congressional authorization—with the president articulating the
governing assumptions—for fuller exploration of policies that
balanced the goals of anticommunism and nuclear war avoidance.

TEST BAN FALLOUT: THE WHEAT DEAL

The extent to which the test ban achievement afforded the
administration greater flexibility in dealing with the Soviets
was demonstrated by the president's decision to allow export
licenses to be granted to wheat dealers interested in trading
with the Soviets—a decision made shortly after Senate ratification of the Test Ban Treaty. Trade policy had been a major
instrument of American Cold War diplomacy since passage
of the Export Control Act in 1949. In 1961 Congress banned
the export of Food for Peace commodities to all Communist
countries except Poland and Yugoslavia and in another action
restricted the sale of subsidized foods to "unfriendly"
countries. In 1962 Congress prohibited the president from
granting most-favored-nation status to all but two Communist states. These statutory measures stemmed from Congress's
deeply held belief that the relaxation of trade restrictions

would ultimately work to the strategic advantage of the Soviet bloc.

According to Secretary of Commerce Luther Hodges, a major participant in the wheat deal decision, Kennedy "felt generally that we ought to have more trade between the Soviets and us."[60] This feeling was accentuated in 1963 with the evolution of détente between the superpowers. Khrushchev, responding to Kennedy's American University address, noted an inconsistency between the president's call for better relations and the continued intransigence of American policy on trade matters. According to the Soviet premier, "Trade is an indicator of good relations between states."[61] Considering the high premium that Soviet leaders put on expanded trade, Kennedy reasoned that the failure of the United States to respond positively to Soviet overtures for grain purchases could lead to a "renewal of the Cold War."[62]

In a sense, then, the decision to allow the sale of wheat to the Soviet Union was linked to the president's interpretation of détente as a series of measures—with arms control as one aspect—designed to foster cooperation in areas of mutual interest to the United States and Soviet Union. The wheat deal, however, represented more than a response to changes in the international situation governing relations between the two countries. Instead it arose in large part from new public expectations about the extent to which previously proscribed transactions with the "enemy" were now legitimate and hence allowable. In a general sense this invested the government with greater freedom to explore avenues for joint Soviet-American cooperation, such as a combined space enterprise. In the specific case of the wheat deal, however, the new climate of opinion allowed agricultural interests with an economic stake in expanded trade to press the government to broaden the scope of sanctioned transactions. Had the government not originally taken the lead in legitimizing mutually beneficial contacts with the Soviets, it is improbable that farmers, given their long tradition of anticommunism and no matter their dire economic circumstances, would have considered trading with the country's principal adversary.

Secretary of Agriculture Orville Freeman informed the cabinet on September 24 that American wheat brokers were in Canada to explore Soviet interest in purchasing grain from American traders.[63] According to Sorensen, Freeman's disclosure ignited a spontaneous discussion, with the secretaries of defense, commerce, labor, and treasury offering their opinions.[64] The next day Kennedy left Washington for a tour of the West and instructed Sorensen to assemble appropriate information. Meanwhile, staff work was conducted within the departments so that by the time Kennedy returned it was "ripe for a presidential decision."[65] On October 1 the president convened the National Security Council along with representatives from the Departments of Agriculture, Justice, Commerce, and the Treasury. According to Under Secretary of Agriculture Charles Murphy, the decision to allow the wheat sale was made on the basis of a one- to two-hour discussion that took place that day.[66] Several days later the president announced his decision after informing key members of Congress two hours beforehand. His opposition in Congress later charged Kennedy with failure to consult Congress adequately. Llewellyn Thompson, who was present at the meeting, was nevertheless quite impressed with the president's handling of the legislators: "He managed skillfully to let anyone speak . . . without getting . . . bound in any way to follow their advice, but at the same time without giving them the impression that their advice had been ignored."[67]

The wheat deal decision was clearly not a presidential initiative despite its intrinsic connection to Kennedy's policy of détente. Instead, according to Senate Majority Leader Mike Mansfield, the president had to be "taught about its importance."[68] Aside from its foreign policy implications, the wheat deal was primarily a domestic issue touching on the concerns and interests of wheat growers, who were principally in the Midwest. It involved complex issues of domestic agricultural policy, and as Murphy recalled, "He [Kennedy] did not have as much detailed knowledge about agricultural programs and agricultural problems as he did in some other fields."[69]

Freeman's advocacy of a wheat transaction with the Soviets resulted from his newfound awareness of major and unanticipated attitudinal changes in the country's Wheat Belt. In mid-September, the agricultural secretary visited Iowa and Kansas and was surprised to hear that farmers were expressing strong interest in trading with the Soviets.[70] This change in sentiment might be attributed to several factors. First, on a purely economic basis, wheat growers quite obviously stood to benefit from the lifting of trade restrictions; it would open a vast new market for export and help to stabilize wheat prices at home. Second, coming on the heels of the Canadian decision to sell $800 million worth of wheat to the Soviets, the change in farm belt attitudes can be

viewed as a case of "emulative linkage," to borrow James
Rosenau's terminology.[71] In the case of the wheat deal, the
decision of the Canadian government, a major Western ally, to
allow the sale of wheat to the Soviets served as a model for
American producers and traders.

Third, and perhaps most important from a political standpoint, there was a general perception by the public, long hostile
to transactions with the Soviets, that conditions had changed
enough to allow for new policies. This attitude was best summed
up by a business leader at a White House Conference held in
mid-September. The conference of 200 businessmen was
spontaneously diverted from its agenda by a call to the president from several businessmen for a reexamination of Soviet
trade policy. When asked why the business community was
suddenly reversing a long and firmly held policy against expanded trade, one businessman was reported to have responded
that "changed world conditions" had produced attitudinal
changes.[72]

The change in attitudes among farmers was, in fact, so remarkable that it astonished even the principal agricultural interest groups in the country. The three most important of these
groups were the Farm Bureau, the Grange, and the National
Association of Wheat Growers.[73] The Farm Bureau, the largest
of the three organizations, represented 1,600,000 families, of
which 10 percent were commercial wheat growers. The Grange
had a membership of 800,000 in the Northeast and Northwest,
most of whom planted some wheat acreage. The National
Association of Wheat Growers represented approximately
70,000 to 75,000 farmers. These farm organizations, which
traditionally had been strongly anti-Communist, were as much
surprised by the shift in farm sentiment as was the administration. Realizing that opposition from among farmers was no
more than a "loud murmur,"[74] both the Grange and National
Farm Bureau promised to reevaluate their traditional hostility
to trade with the Soviet Union and offered to submit the
issue to their respective memberships.

While farm support was clearly an important resource in the
president's attempt to dramatize the wheat deal as a major
step in the continuing Soviet-American détente, Kennedy was
reluctant to act unilaterally without congressional authorization. Despite its domestic features, the wheat issue touched
on a sacred tenet of postwar American foreign policy. As far
as Congress was concerned, any transaction that alleviated

pressure on the Soviet economy would ultimately allow the Soviets to concentrate their energies and resources on further development of their strategic capabilities. The Republican party, in particular, had accepted the test ban as a measure that did not violate the essential goal of anticommunism. Trading with the enemy, however, not only suggested a more cooperative relationship with communism but also appeared to violate numerous congressional resolutions and statutes limiting such transactions. Kennedy felt vulnerable on this issue and with elections around the corner, wanted to secure bipartisan support for his initiative.

In reality, most administration supporters argued that the wheat deal did not require specific congressional authorization. The Justice Department supported this contention,[75] and in a discussion with Senator Aiken, the president was advised not to seek legislation where it was unnecessary.[76] Nevertheless, Kennedy wanted to prevent the Republicans from making the wheat deal into a campaign issue. With Vice-President Lyndon Johnson referring to the decision as "the worst political mistake we have made in foreign policy in this administration,"[77] the president dispatched Secretaries Hodges and Freeman along with Assistant Secretary George Ball to lobby with the House Foreign Affairs and Agriculture Committees. Instead of gaining support, however, the disclosure of administration intentions mobilized Republican opposition. This prompted political aide Dutton to request that the administration cease its consultations with Congressional committees: "When no legislative action is required, as for the wheat sale, the executive branch triggers opposition by seeking a broad expression of legislative support."[78]

Kennedy's calculated political approach to the wheat sale issue did not initially materialize as he had hoped. Instead of developing a strong bipartisan consensus behind the deal, it mobilized much opposition from Republicans, even among those from wheat-producing states. To Republicans, the issue was not just wheat but also the alleged usurpation of congressional authority by presidential fiat. Kennedy was cognizant of this controversy in announcing his approval of such sales on October 9. He defended the administration's decision not to prohibit private wheat sales to the Soviet Union and then asserted that despite the absence of any need for congressional authorization, he would still refer his action to Congress.[79]

The president, upon sensing the difficulties in attempting to build bipartisan congressional support for the wheat sale, decided to employ the same tactics that had worked so well in the case of the test ban. One of the most effective of these measures was simply independent presidential action. On October 9, despite the absence of widespread Republican support, the president announced his decision to the nation; if he could not win Congress, as he had initially attempted to do, he would circumvent it. Afterwards, Kennedy began to build public support on behalf of his initiative. Noting the link between the wheat deal and test ban, Kennedy enlisted the aid of groups that had helped in the treaty effort. He also supplied favorably inclined congressmen with supportive speeches and statistics and intervened to win the support of potentially hostile groups, such as Polish-Americans and longshoremen. The final resolution of the debate in Congress did not occur until after his death, but eventually, the deal succeeded without statutory interference from the legislative branch.

THE TEST BAN TREATY AND THE WHEAT DEAL COMPARED

The wheat deal, besides being one aspect of détente, was far different, both in character and policy-making development, from the test ban issue. For one thing, it touched on the occupational concerns of farmers and longshoremen and hence represented a much sharper confluence of domestic and foreign policy interests. As a consequence, the scope and intensity of interest group involvement was much greater than in the case of the Test Ban Treaty. Another difference involved the extent to which each issue experienced presidential input. While Kennedy ultimately made both decisions, the test ban issue evolved over a much longer period of time with a significantly greater degree of direct presidential participation. In the test ban case, the president had to intervene frequently to insure that the policy-making direction of his administration conformed to his preferences. In the case of the wheat deal, while presidential actions were instrumental in making the sale a reality, the initiative originated and ultimately developed in the bureaucracy. By the time Kennedy was called upon to make a decision, it had already developed a governmental consensus.

The president, in pushing for a test ban, was essentially continuing, albeit more deftly and with greater resolution, a policy that his Republican predecessor had initiated. When presented to the Republicans for ratification, the issue already had built-in bipartisan support. In the case of the wheat deal, Kennedy was

moving in entirely new directions—directions, in fact, that
Republicans had consistently opposed in the past. Bipartisan
support in this case was not immediately forthcoming, particularly because Republicans like Richard Nixon sensed that this
was an issue out of which political capital could be generated.

The Test Ban Treaty required a public examination because
of the constitutional prerogative assigned to the Senate. The
wheat deal, however, did not necessarily require congressional
ratification, although opponents claimed that it did. Kennedy's
decision to submit it for consideration represented his attempt
to defuse it as a potential election issue. Advisers such as
Fred Dutton argued that, on the contrary, by opening the issue
to congressional debate, Kennedy was creating a problem where
one did not necessarily exist.

Despite these significant differences, the two issues must be
considered in tandem. For one thing, both were part of a policy
of détente and hence tied to Kennedy's view of Soviet-American
relations. Second, and perhaps most important, the wheat deal
would not, in all probability, have occurred in the absence of
the test ban agreement. In some respects, this means that without the prior, positive achievement in Soviet-American relations,
other developments, such as the wheat deal, would have never
materialized. Considering the symbolic political importance of
the test ban as a barometer of Cold War tensions, the collapse
of test ban negotiations would have probably signaled a deterioration in all areas of mutual concern. Senator Stephen Young of
Ohio was cognizant of this fact when in August he urged the
administration to take advantage of the new mood in Soviet-
American relations to look into the possibilities of expanded
trade.[80]

At the same time, the new climate in relations was matched
by a greater domestic receptivity to the undertaking of positive
transactions between the two countries. The administration
"broke the ice" by signaling to the public that certain types of
transactions, based on mutual interest, could indeed be legitimate. Once this occurred, not only did it afford Kennedy
a more conducive domestic environment for the further pursuit
of détente, but it also induced groups perceiving a potential advantage in dealing with the Soviets to reevaluate the attitudes
and policy preferences that had become a staple of Cold War
diplomacy. Thus, the events of 1963 had great impact not only
on government policy but on public attitudes and behavior as
they related both to their own interests and more generally
toward relations with the Soviet Union.

NOTES

1. Hazel Gaudet Erskine, "The Polls: Kennedy as President," *Public Opinion Quarterly* 28 (Summer 1964): 334-35.

2. *The New York Times,* 30 January 1963, p. 2.

3. *The New York Times,* 1 March 1963, p. 1.

4. *The New York Times,* 1 February 1963, p. 1. Hosmer's stridency was reflected in the generally abusive tone he employed to question government witnesses in their testimony before the Joint Committee on Atomic Energy. U.S., Congress, Joint Committee on Atomic Energy, *Hearings: Developments in Technical Capabilities for the Detection and Inspection of Nuclear Tests,* 88th Cong., 1st sess., 1963.

5. *The New York Times,* 11 February 1963, p. 1.

6. *The New York Times,* 19 March 1963, p. 1.

7. *The New York Times,* 22 February 1963, p. 1.

8. U.S., Congress, Senate, Committee on Armed Services, Preparedness Investigating Subcommittee, *Hearings: Military Aspects and Implications of Nuclear Test Ban Proposals and Related Matters,* 88th Cong., 1st sess., 1963, pp. 21-49, passim.

9. Memorandum, Theodore Sorensen to President John F. Kennedy, January 25, 1962, John F. Kennedy Library.

10. Memorandum, Frederick Dutton, John F. Kennedy Library.

11. Sidney Kraus, Reuben Mehling, and Elaine El-Assal, "Mass Media and the Fallout Controversy," *Public Opinion Quarterly* 27 (Summer 1963): 191-205.

12. Mary Milling Lepper, *Foreign Policy Formulation: A Case Study of the Nuclear Test Ban Treaty* (Columbus, Ohio: Charles E. Merrill, 1971), p. 78.

13. Ibid., p. 94.

14. *The New York Times,* 4 March 1963, p. 1.

15. U.S., President, *Public Papers of the Presidents of the United States,* (Washington, D.C.: U.S. Government Printing Office), John F. Kennedy, 1963, p. 208.

16. *Public Papers . . . Kennedy, 1963,* p. 280.

17. Theodore C. Sorensen, *Kennedy* (New York: Harper and Row, 1965), p. 310.

18. *Public Papers . . . Kennedy, 1962,* p. 141.

19. George F. Kennan, recorded interview by Louis Fischer, March 23, 1965, pp. 43-44. John F. Kennedy Library Oral History Program.

20. Theodore Sorensen, recorded interviews by Carl Kaysen, March 26, 1964, and April 4, 1964, p. 72. John F. Kennedy Library Oral History Program.

21. *The New York Times,* 22 July 1963, p. 2.

22. *Public Papers . . . Kennedy, 1963,* p. 609.

23. Norman Cousins, *The Improbable Triumvirate* (New York: Norton, 1972), p. 128.

24. *Public Papers . . . Kennedy, 1963,* p. 609.

25. *The New York Times,* 8 April 1963, p. 46.

26. *The New York Times,* 17 July 1963, p. 2.

27. Sorensen, *Kennedy,* p. 739.

28. Cousins, *The Improbable Triumvirate,* p. 138-44.

29. Ibid., p. 129.

30. Ibid., p. 127.

31. Robert A. Dahl, *Congress and Foreign Policy* (New York: Norton, 1950), p. 35.

32. *The New York Times*, 19 September 1963, p. 10.

33. Arthur M. Schlesinger, Jr., *A Thousand Days* (Boston: Houghton Mifflin, 1965; Fawcett, 1967), p. 831.

34. Lepper, *Foreign Policy Formulation*, p. 51.

35. Ibid., p. 54.

36. Schlesinger, *A Thousand Days*, p. 443.

37. Erskine, "The Polls," pp. 338-39.

38. Sorensen, *Kennedy*, p. 733.

39. *Newsweek*, 8 July 1963, p. 21.

40. Erskine, "The Polls," p. 336.

41. Max Frankel, "A Silence in Washington," *The New York Times*, 25 July 1963, p. 2.

42. *Newsweek*, 26 August 1963, pp. 25-27.

43. *The New York Times*, 12 August 1963, p. 1.

44. *Newsweek*, 5 August 1963, p. 17.

45. Mike Mansfield, recorded interview by Seth P. Tillman, June 23, 1964, p. 16. John F. Kennedy Library Oral History Program.

46. Sorensen, *Kennedy*, p. 737.

47. Benjamin H. Read, recorded interviews by Joseph E. O'Connor and Dennis O'Brien, February 22, 1966, and October 17, 1969, p. 12. John F. Kennedy Library Oral History Program.

48. *Public Papers . . . Kennedy, 1963*, pp. 669-71.

49. U.S., Arms Control and Disarmament Agency, *Documents on Disarmament, 1963*, p. 497.

50. *The New York Times*, 11 June 1963, p. 17.

51. *Public Papers . . . Kennedy, 1962*, p. 779.

52. *The New York Times*, 6 August 1963, p. 14.

53. James A. Robinson, *Congress and Foreign Policy-Making* (Homewood, Ill.: Dorsey Press, 1967), p. vii.

54. Cecil V. Crabb, Jr., *Foreign Policy in the Nuclear Age* (New York: Harper and Row, 1972), p. 106.

55. Aaron Wildavsky, *The Revolt Against the Masses and Other Essays on Politics and Public Policy* (New York and London: Basic Books, 1971), p. 326.

56. Ibid., p. 324.

57. *Hearings: Military Aspects . . .* , p. 800.

58. *The New York Times*, 20 October 1963, p. 1.

59. Harold Macmillan, *At the End of the Day: 1961-1963*, (New York: Harper and Row, 1973), p. 455.

60. Luther H. Hodges, recorded interviews by Dan Jacobs, March 19, 1964, and March 21, 1964, p. 93. John F. Kennedy Library Oral History Program.

61. *Documents on Disarmament, 1963*, p. 223.

62. *The New York Times*, 11 October 1963, p. 1.

63. Mansfield interview, p. 32.

64. Sorensen, *Kennedy*, p. 740.

65. Charles Murphy, recorded interview by George A. Barnes, June 30, 1964, p. 28. John F. Kennedy Library Oral History Program.

66. Ibid., p. 27.

67. Llewellyn Thompson, recorded interviews by Elizabeth Donahue, March 25, 1964, and Joseph E. O'Connor, April 27, 1966, p. 9. John F. Kennedy Library Oral History Program.

68. Mansfield interview, p. 32.

69. Murphy interview, p. 15.

70. *The New York Times*, 20 September 1963, p. 10.

71. James N. Rosenau, *Linkage Politics* (New York: Free Press, 1969), p. 46.

72. *The New York Times*, 19 September 1963, p. 14.

73. *The New York Times*, 22 September 1963, p. 1.

74. *The New York Times*, 20 September 1963, p. 10.

75. Memorandum, Assistant Attorney General Norbert A. Schlei to Theodore C. Sorensen, September 27, 1963, Sorensen Files, John F. Kennedy Library.

76. Mansfield interview, p. 16.

77. Schlesinger, *A Thousand Days*, p. 840.

78. Memorandum, Frederick Dutton to McGeorge Bundy and Larry O'Brien, September 30, 1963, National Security Files, John F. Kennedy Library.

79. *Public Papers . . . Kennedy, 1963*, p. 767.

80. *The New York Times*, 21 August 1963, p. 34.

7.
EPILOGUE

The spirit of détente that the successful negotiation and ratification of the Test Ban Treaty offered engendered hope in some
administration officials for a meaningful de-escalation of the
arms race. Between August and November Kennedy and Rusk
met with Soviet Foreign Minister Andrei Gromyko and Ambassador Dobrynin to explore the feasibility of mutual force reductions in Europe. Following the president's assassination, the
Johnson administration, still staffed largely by Kennedy hold-
overs, announced the withdrawal of 8,000 troops from Europe.
This initiative was met by a Soviet withdrawal of 14,000
troops from East Germany and a cutback in naval construction.
According to Schlesinger, this experiment in reciprocal arms
control came to an end with Khrushchev's ouster in October
1964 and the coming to power of a new hard-line group in
the Kremlin.[1]

Schlesinger's account of these post-Test Ban Treaty initiatives suggests that the Kennedy administration was moving in
the direction of a fresh arms control approach. Prior to 1963,
the administration's arms control policy depended on a simultaneous expansion in the nation's nuclear and conventional
capabilities. With both the Cuban crisis and test ban behind
him, however, Kennedy hoped to explore a form of arms control that would result in reductions in armaments on both sides.
Rather than implement the policy through formal treaty—
which would only embroil the president in protracted debate
with his military and hard-line elements on Capitol Hill—arms
control could be achieved through reciprocal, unilateral
initiatives. That this never occurred on any significant scale can

be attributed in part to Kennedy's death, Khrushchev's dramatic fall from power, and the worsening of the Viet Nam situation.

In retrospect, one wonders whether the Kennedy détente was as contemporaneously significant as many portrayed it to be and whether it provided any legitimate promise for arresting the arms spiral. On the contrary, one might argue, the Kennedy program of military spending during the first two years of his administration coupled with the Soviet humiliation over Cuba had the long-range effect of accelerating and intensifying the Soviet arms buildup. Before the end of the decade, the United States and the Soviet Union reached a level of rough nuclear parity, changing not only the strategic equation between them but also the terms under which détente and arms control could be pursued.

The long-range utility of the Test Ban Treaty is also questionable. Since 1963 the number of experimental nuclear blasts underground has exceeded the total number of underground *and* atmospheric detonations prior to the treaty. Finally, whereas the spirit of détente promised a relaxation in political tensions between the superpowers, the Cold War continued to oscillate between periods of relative calm and high tension. The limits of détente, according to Schlesinger, were made starkly clear to the president several weeks before his death when the Soviets detained an American professor in Moscow as a spy.[2]

What, then, was the legacy of the Kennedy administration? Was it to fuel the arms race and sharpen the interventionist tendencies in American foreign policy, as critics have charged? Or was it to offer a brief moment of respite from the cycle of suspicion and mutual confrontation, which had until then rigidified each country's approach to the Cold War? It is difficult to speculate on what might have been had Kennedy lived beyond November 1963 and had Khrushchev survived the coup of 1964. Most probably, the Soviet-American approach to the fundamental question of nuclear weapons would not have been demonstrably different from what evolved under Kennedy's successors. Owing to the objective nature of Soviet-American relations and to the intense pressures of domestic and bureaucratic politics, the range of choice available to presidents, as already demonstrated, is fairly circumscribed. For Kennedy to achieve more than an incremental amelioration of the Cold War would have required a remarkable and

fortuitous confluence of international and domestic changes.
On the other hand—and here speculation takes over—had there
been no significant escalation of the war in Viet Nam and had
Kennedy won an overwhelming electoral victory against
Barry Goldwater in 1964, the domestic parameters around
the president might have been elasticized to the point where
arms control efforts could have been directed toward the
reduction rather than the expansion of armaments.

Speculation notwithstanding, it would be incorrect to minimize the achievements of the Kennedy administration in producing a more favorable setting for the conduct of superpower
relations. For one thing, by producing a negotiated treaty—
as cautious as it was—the administration helped to institutionalize those collaborative aspects of U.S.-Soviet relations that
were to form the basis for future relations between the nuclear
giants. Second, the administration paved the way for the
future integration of arms control considerations into defense
policy—something that Eisenhower, despite his good intentions, could not or would not do. Nixon's acceptance of nuclear
parity and his vigorous pursuit of SALT six years after
Kennedy's death underscores the extent to which mutual deterrence remediated by arms control ultimately evolved into
the foundation of U.S. nuclear strategy—at least until the advent of the Reagan administration. Finally, and not the least
important, Kennedy attempted to educate the public to the
viewpoint that ambivalences in American foreign policy were
legitimate expressions of the national interest.

The last aspect of Kennedy's performance is extremely
significant, for ultimately the domestic political system
governs the extent to which presidents can exploit perceived
opportunities for a relaxation of tensions between the superpowers. To be sure, presidential power in the area of foreign
policy has changed considerably since Kennedy's day.
Kennedy operated from a position of nuclear superiority. His
successors have presided over a steady erosion in U.S. nuclear
might vis-à-vis the Soviet Union. This loss of strategic superiority has not only reduced American leverage over the Soviet
Union but has also made it increasingly difficult for presidents
to justify arms control to their domestic constituencies. Nixon,
for example, was forced after 1972 to negotiate equal ceilings
on nuclear weapons despite Nixon's view that Soviet advantages
in numbers were more than offset by American qualitative
superiority. Ford, beset by political problems in 1976, put

SALT negotiations on the back burner and deliberately
avoided using the word "détente" despite his inclination to
continue Nixon's policies. Carter, operating in an environment
where Soviet technological advances challenged even the existence of nuclear parity, found it ever more difficult to sell
arms control at home without drastically increasing expenditures in the defense field. And even then it was not enough to
convince the public that the United States had not lost a
critical edge in its dealings with the Soviet Union. And in
1980 a president was elected who was openly skeptical about
the value of arms control.

Strategic changes are not alone, however, in limiting presidential leeway. The 1970s produced a serious enervation of
the institutional presidency. Watergate and Viet Nam contributed to the decline while simultaneously generating a
reawakening of congressional assertiveness in the area of foreign
policy. Measures such as the War Powers and Case-Zablocki
Acts were designed to shrink presidential prerogatives in the
area of war making and in the negotiation of executive agreements. Other measures proscribing the president from allocat-
ing aid to pro-U.S. factions and governments in South Viet
Nam, Angola, and Turkey made it difficult for presidents to
maneuver in a way that the Cold War had accustomed them to.
In sum, these and other measures like them were designed to
impinge on the freedom that presidents had traditionally enjoyed in pursuing the goal of anticommunism. In the late
1970s the pendulum in Congress shifted toward a renewed
commitment to arrest the spread of communism. While this
sentiment was clearly distinguishable from the antidefense
feeling that led to congressional reassertion in the 1970s, the
tendency to challenge presidential predominance in the area
of foreign policy remained. This made the job of selling
détente all the more difficult.

The resurgence of congressional power was in no small part
derivative of a fraying of the national consensus that had
guided American foreign policy since the end of World War
II. In Kennedy's day the guidelines by which presidents conducted the Cold War were fairly clear. The Cold War was perceived as a military and political confrontation between two
antithetical ideological camps who nevertheless could be expected to forego ideology in pursuit of a mutual objective—
nuclear war avoidance. Even Johnson, who was much more
dogmatically oriented against communism than his predecessor,

accepted these basic premises and sought to negotiate with
the Soviet Union. The Viet Nam disaster, however, and the
obvious disintegration of the Communist bloc called into
question the premise that the U.S. response to communism
should have such a decidedly military cast. Thus, in the 1970s
the middle-marginal consensus began to break down in favor
of an approach that emphasized reductions in defense spending and U.S. military involvement overseas. But this approach
produced a counterreaction from those who viewed with
alarm the buildup of Soviet military might and the apparent
slackening of U.S. military and diplomatic resolve. To critics
from the right, this dangerous combination indicated that the
Soviets no longer had to view nuclear war with such trepida-
tion. The major difference between the domestic situation in
the 1960s and that of the late 1970s and the early 1980s is
the absence of a firm middle ground in the latter period.
Today, the foreign policy debate has become polarized between two marginalist extremes—with the anti-Communists
presently in command. In the 1960s, presidents, who naturally
occupied the middle ground, enjoyed the support of a large
middle-marginal constituency. Today, the middle ground is
caught between the conflicting pressures of antiwar and anti-
Communist marginalism. The middle ground, which favors a
strong military response to communism in conjunction with
arms control, has shrunk dramatically.

These important differences between the foreign policy
setting today and the one that existed during Kennedy's time
obviously indicate the limits of the case study approach to
understanding Cold War American diplomacy. Nevertheless,
the Kennedy case is instructive in a number of ways. For one
thing, it serves by comparison as a basis for understanding the
extent to which American foreign policy has changed over the
last twenty years. Moreover, in reviewing the record of foreign
policy debate over the Test Ban Treaty, one is struck by the
prominence of certain factors that recur even today. One of
these features is the relatively persistent interplay of bureaucratic forces in favor of and opposed to arms control. The
Eisenhower administration was the first to mobilize these
forces into any coherent pattern. Since then, and particularly
since the advent of the ACDA, the policy-making process has
evolved a fairly stable pattern of in-fighting and compromise.
Generally, the ACDA and State Department have favored arms
control initiatives, whereas the military has been relatively

restrained, if not openly hostile, toward these efforts. The inevitability of bureaucratic and personal debate in this area usually produces policies that are carefully tailored to meet all sides of the question.

At the same time, the decision-making system does not crank out arms control policies without significant central direction. The tendency of those who favor arms control to push ahead relentlessly and for those opposed to impede their efforts means that the policy-making system has the potential either for stalemate or for striking out in dramatically contradictory directions. A president must, therefore, work hard to produce a coherent arms control policy. As noted above, the Eisenhower administration's test ban policy suffered from a lack of presidential direction. The Kennedy administration, on the other hand, experienced the exact reverse. The president was willing to compromise but also willing to circumvent those who opposed him. Johnson tended to seek compromise by devising ingenious face-saving formulas, as in the case of the ABM. His successor adopted a different approach. Nixon concentrated power in a trusted lieutenant and conducted real negotiations through a "back channel." The Ford administration is difficult to assess both because it was so short and because its principal protagonists essentially continued the patterns of interaction that had developed under Nixon—with Kissinger as the principal agent of foreign policy. Nevertheless, Ford did step in to protect Kissinger from the obstructionism of Defense Secretary Schlesinger. As Kissinger's domestic standing began to sag, however, he became more vulnerable to opposition from the Joint Chiefs of Staff and a close Ford confidant, the new defense secretary, Donald Rumsfeld. At this juncture, negotiations with the Soviets stalled, primarily because the president was not willing to intercede on behalf of his secretary of state as he had done several months earlier. At times, Carter allowed the split in his administration between Secretary of State Cyrus Vance and NSC Chief Brzezinski to flare publicly. Nevertheless, in the case of SALT II, the president's intense involvement in policy formulation had a decided effect in reconciling intrabureaucratic disputes all along the way. It is clear that when a president does not have a commitment to arms control, it will be next to impossible for bureaucratic advocates of arms control to succeed.

Another feature of the Kennedy détente that applies to other administrations is the primacy of domestic political con-

siderations in the construction of arms control policy. This is
not to say that the character of the domestic setting does not
change over time or that certain presidents operate in more
constricted environments than others. Nevertheless, the success
or failure of arms control policy depends, in large part, on the
president's ability to sell the policy as a legitimate pursuit of
the national interest. Kennedy was especially sensitive to this
need, and one can easily trace his decision to seek a limited
rather than a comprehensive ban to the exigencies of domestic
politics. The Nixon case is somewhat different. Nixon, because
of his strong anti-Communist credentials, was able to neutralize
the right wing. At the same time, Nixon had to contend with
pressures from Congress that the president felt undermined his
ability to gain concessions from the Soviets. He did so in part
by meeting some of the concerns of the antiwar lobby on
Capitol Hill through reductions in defense expenditures.
Nixon also differed from Kennedy in his approach to political
mobilization. Kennedy used his rhetorical skills and personal
involvement in managing supportive interest group activity to
gain acceptance for the Test Ban Treaty. Nixon, however, gained
support for his initiatives—such as the opening to China—by
undertaking dramatic, unilateral actions. The Carter performance
is difficult to evaluate because of the change in the domestic
setting over the last few years. Carter was faulted for not consult-
ing Congress in a proper manner, for allowing bipartisanship
to fade, and for leaving the field of arms control debate to
those opposed to his efforts.[3] Moreover, by canceling projects
such as the B-1 bomber and suspending development of the
neutron bomb, he left himself open to charges that he was
soft on communism. Nevertheless, there are indications that
in framing his SALT II policy, Carter was attempting to satisfy
certain interests on Capitol Hill. His appointment of a military
man to head the ACDA and his decision to develop and deploy
the MX missile were clearly governed by political considerations. Some may argue that these measures were clumsy efforts
to recoup from earlier mistakes. Nevertheless, given the character of the political environment in which Carter operated,
it is questionable whether any political concession on his part
would have satisfactorily satisfied the public mood and simultaneously produced an effective arms control policy.

Perhaps the greatest link between the Kennedy presidency
and those of his successors is the continuing primacy of the
Soviet Union in American foreign policy calculations. Many

commentators, responding to the close of the Viet Nam War, the mid-1970s oil crisis, and the relative institutionalization of détente, speculated that the traditional Cold War American concern with the Soviet Union would recede in favor of a greater preoccupation with revolutionary change in the Third World. Indeed, the Carter administration took office with similar assumptions about the world situation. Time, however, has proven the resiliency of the anti-Soviet theme in the American approach to its interests abroad. That this is so is in no small part attributable to the continuing strength of anti-Communist sentiment among significant elements of the bureaucracy and the electorate. At the same time, it is impossible to escape the conclusion that the American preoccupation with Soviet power is grounded in a fairly realistic assessment of the exigencies of a still bipolar, albeit more complex, international system. The landscape and terms of conflict between the superpowers have changed, but the threat that they alone pose to one another is as deadly, if not more deadly, than in the past.

Once Kennedy took office, he was motivated to fashion fresh modalities by which anticommunism could be pursued without thrusting the world into a nuclear holocaust. This approach guided his successors as they sought to enhance the national interest in the face of a changing strategic equation. The true test of presidential power and imagination in the coming decade will be not only to forge an effective strategy to deal with the Soviet threat to America's global interests but also to revive a national consensus that accepts the ambivalent character of the national interest. Kennedy's major contribution was to assert the legitimacy of this ambivalence.

NOTES

1. Private correspondence, Arthur M. Schlesinger, Jr., to the author, April 23, 1979.

2. Arthur M. Schlesinger, Jr., *A Thousand Days* (Boston: Houghton Mifflin, 1965; Fawcett, 1967), p. 842.

3. See Alton Frye and William D. Rodgers, "Linkage Begins at Home," *Foreign Policy* 35 (Summer 1979): 49-67. See also George S. McGovern, "Seize the Initiative," *Foreign Policy* 39 (Summer 1980): 3-5.

BIBLIOGRAPHY

MAJOR ARCHIVES

John F. Kennedy Library, Boston, Massachusetts

President's Office Files
National Security Files
Transition Files, 1960-61
Arthur Schlesinger Files
Theodore Sorensen Files

Oral History Interviews, John F. Kennedy Oral History Program

Charles E. Bohlen, recorded interview by Arthur M. Schlesinger, Jr., May 21, 1964.
Abram Chayes, recorded interview by Eugene Gordon, May 18, June 22-23, 1964.
Adrian Fisher, recorded interview by Frank Sieverts, May 13, 1964.
W. Averell Harriman, recorded interview by Michael W. Forrestal, April 13, 1964.
Luther H. Hodges, recorded interview by Dan Jacobs, March 19, 21, 1964.
U. Alexis Johnson, recorded interview by William Brubeck, 1964.
George F. Kennan, recorded interview by Louis Fischer, March 23, 1965.
Nikita S. Khrushchev, oral history interview conducted on June 29, 1964.
Mike Mansfield, recorded interview by Seth P. Tillman, June 23, 1964.
Charles Murphy, recorded interview by George A. Barnes, June 30, 1964.
Benjamin H. Read, recorded interview by Joseph E. O'Conner and Dennis O'Brien, February 22, 1966 and October 17, 1969.
Theodore C. Sorensen, recorded interview by Carl Kaysen, March 26, April 4, 1964.
Llewellyn Thompson, recorded interview by Elizabeth Donahue, March

23, 1964 and Joseph E. O'Conner, April 27, 1966.
Earle Wheeler, recorded interview by Chester Clifton, 1964.
Herbert York, recorded interview by Steven Rivkin, June 16, 1964.

CONGRESSIONAL DOCUMENTS

U.S. Congress. House. Committee on Armed Services. *Hearings on Military Posture.* 88th Congress, 1st session, 1963.

U.S. Congress. House. Committee on Foreign Affairs. *Hearings on Bill to Establish a U.S. Arms Control Agency.* 87th Congress, 1st session, 1961.

U.S. Congress. Joint Committee on Atomic Energy. *Hearings: Developments in Technical Capabilities for the Detection and Inspection of Nuclear Tests.* 88th Congress, 1st session, 1963.

U.S. Congress. Senate. Committee on Armed Services. Preparedness Investigating Subcommittee. *Hearings: Military Aspects and Implications of Nuclear Test Ban Treaty and Related Proposals.* 88th Congress, 1st session, 1963.

U.S. Congress. Senate. Committee on Armed Services. Preparedness Investigating Subcommittee. *Interim Report—Investigation of the Preparedness Program.* 88th Congress, 1st session, 1963.

U.S. Congress. Senate. Committee on Commerce. Subcommittee of the Committee on Communications. *The Speeches, Remarks, Press Conferences, and Statements of Senator John F. Kennedy, August 1 Through November 7, 1960.* 87th Congress, 1st session, 1961.

U.S. Congress. Senate. Committee on Foreign Relations. *Hearings: Disarmament Agency-S. 2180-A Bill to Establish a United States Disarmament Agency for World Peace and Security.* 87th Congress, 1st session, 1961.

U.S. Congress. Senate. Committee on Foreign Relations. *Hearings: Nuclear Test Ban Treaty.* 88th Congress, 1st session, 1963.

GOVERNMENT DOCUMENTS

Bundy, McGeorge. "The Next Steps Toward Peace: Some Notes on the Two-Legged Process." *Department of State Bulletin* 49 (October 21, 1963): 625-30.

Dean, Arthur H. "United States Considers Question of Suspension of Nuclear and Thermonuclear Tests." *Department of State Bulletin* 47 (November 26, 1962): 817-24.

Foster, William C. "The Nuclear Test Ban Issue." *Department of State Bulletin* 48 (March 18, 1963): 398-402.

Public Papers of the Presidents: John F. Kennedy, 1961-1963. Washington, D.C.: United States Government Printing Office, 1962-1964.

U.S. Arms Control and Disarmament Agency. *Documents on Disarmament.* 1960-1963. 5 volumes. Washington, D.C.: Government Printing Office, 1961-1964.

U.S. Department of State. *Department of State Bulletin* 49, no. 1795 (November 19, 1973): 635-55.

U.S. Department of State. *United States Treaties and Other International Agreements.* Washington, D.C.: United States Government Printing Office, 1964.

BOOKS

Acheson, Dean. *Present at the Creation: My Years in the State Department.* New York: New American Library, 1970.

Allison, Graham. *Essence of Decision.* Boston: Little, Brown, 1971.

Almond, Gabriel A. *The American People and Foreign Policy.* 2d ed. New York: Praeger, 1960.

Ambrose, Stephen E. *Rise to Globalism: American Foreign Policy Since 1938.* London: Allen Lane, Penguin Press, 1971.

Armacost, Michael H. *The Politics of Weapons Innovation: The Thor Jupiter Controversy.* New York and London: Columbia University Press, 1969.

Aron, Raymond. *The Imperial Republic: The United States and the World 1945-1973.* Englewood Cliffs, N.J.: Prentice-Hall, 1974.

———. *Peace and War: A Theory of International Relations.* Garden City, N.Y.: Doubleday, 1966.

Art, Robert J. *The TFX Decision.* Boston: Little, Brown, 1968.

Bacchus, William I. *Foreign Policy and the Bureaucratic Process.* Princeton, N.J.: Princeton University Press, 1974.

Barber, James David. *The Presidential Character: Predicting Performance in the White House.* Englewood Cliffs, N.J.: Prentice-Hall, 1977.

Barnet, Richard. *Intervention and Revolution.* Cleveland, Ohio, and New York: The World Publishing Co., 1968.

———. *Roots of War.* New York: Atheneum, 1972.

Bechhoefer, Bernhard G. *Postwar Negotiations for Arms Control.* Washington, D.C.: Brookings Institution, 1961.

Bernstein, Barton, ed. *Politics and Policies of the Truman Administration.* Chicago: Quadrangle, 1970.

Binkley, Wilfred Ellsworth. *President and Congress.* 3d. rev. ed. New York: Vintage, 1962.

Bloomfield, Lincoln Palmer. *Disarmament and Arms Control.* New York: Foreign Policy Association, 1968.

Bottome, Edgar M. *The Missile Gap: A Study of the Formulation of Military and Political Policy.* Teaneck, N.J.: Fairleigh Dickinson University Press, 1971.

Boulding, Kenneth E. *The Image.* Ann Arbor, Mich.: The University of Michigan Press, 1956.

Bradlee, Benjamin C. *Conversations with Kennedy.* New York: W. W. Norton, 1975; Pocket Books, 1976.

Brennan, Donald G. *Arms Control, Disarmament and National Security.* New York: G. Braziller, 1961.

Brodie, Bernard. *Strategy in the Missile Age.* Princeton, N.J.: Princeton University Press, 1959.

Brown, Seyom. *The Faces of Power.* New York and London: Columbia University Press, 1968.

Burns, James MacGregor. *Presidential Government: The Crucible of Leadership.* Boston: Houghton Mifflin, 1966.

Campbell, John Franklin. *The Foreign Affairs Fudge Factory.* New York and London: Basic Books, 1971.

Clark, Keith C., and Legere, Laurence J. *The President and the Management of National Security: A Report.* New York: Praeger, 1969.

Clemens, Walter C. *The Superpowers and Arms Control: From Cold War to Interdependence.* Lexington, Mass.: Lexington Books, 1973.

Cochran, Charles L. *Civil-Military Relations: Changing Concepts in the Seventies.* New York: The Free Press, 1974.

Cohen, Bernard C. *The Political Process and Foreign Policy: The Making of the Japanese Peace Settlement.* Princeton, N.J.: Princeton University Press, 1957.

——. *The Public's Impact on Foreign Policy.* Boston: Little, Brown, 1973.

Cornwell, Elmer E., Jr. *Presidential Leadership of Public Opinion.* Bloomington, Ind.: Indiana University Press, 1965.

Corwin, Edward. *The President: Office and Powers, 1787-1957.* 4th ed. New York: New York University Press, 1957.

Cottam, Richard W. *Foreign Policy Motivation: A General Theory and a Case Study.* Pittsburgh, Pa.: University of Pittsburgh Press, 1977.

Cousins, Norman. *The Improbable Triumvirate.* New York: W. W. Norton, 1972.

Crabb, Cecil V., Jr. *American Foreign Policy in the Nuclear Age.* New York: Harper and Row, 1972.

——. *Policy-Makers and Critics: Conflicting Theories of American Foreign Policy.* New York: Praeger, 1976.

Cronin, Thomas E., and Greenberg, Sanford D., eds. *The Presidential Advisory System.* New York: Harper and Row, 1969.

Cyert, Richard, and March, James. *A Behavioral Theory of the Firm.* Englewood Cliffs, N.J.: Prentice-Hall, 1963.

Dahl, Robert A. *Congress and Foreign Policy.* New York: W. W. Norton, 1950.

David, James W., Jr. *The National Executive Branch.* New York: The Free Press, 1970.

de Rivera, Joseph H. *The Psychological Dimension of Foreign Policy.* Columbus, Ohio: Charles E. Merrill Publishing Co., 1968.

Destler, I. M. *Presidents, Bureaucrats and Foreign Policy.* Princeton, N.J.: Princeton University Press, 1972.

Divine, Robert. *Foreign Policy and U.S. Presidential Elections.* New York: Franklin Watts, 1974.

Downs, Anthony. *Inside Bureaucracy.* Boston: Little, Brown, 1967.

Dulles, Eleanor Lansing, and Crane, Robert Dickson. *Detente: Cold War Strategies in Transition.* New York: Praeger, 1965.

Emmerich, Herbert. *Federal Organization and Administrative Management.* University, Ala.: University of Alabama Press, 1971.

Enthoven, Alain C. and Smith, K. Wayne. *How Much Is Enough? Shaping
the Defense Program, 1961-1969.* New York: Harper and Row, 1971.

Festinger, Leon. *A Theory of Cognitive Dissonance.* Stanford, Calif.:
Stanford University Press, 1957.

Finer, Herman. *The Presidency: Crisis and Regeneration.* Chicago: University of Chicago Press, 1960.

Finer, S. E. *The Man on Horseback: The Role of the Military in Politics.*
New York: Praeger, 1962.

Fisher, Louis. *President and Congress: Power and Policy.* New York:
The Free Press, 1972.

FitzSimons, Louise. *The Kennedy Doctrine.* New York: Random House,
1972.

Frankel, Joseph. *The Making of Foreign Policy.* London: Oxford University Press, 1963.

Gaddis, John Lewis. *The United States and the Origins of the Cold War.*
New York: Columbia University Press, 1972.

Galbraith, John Kenneth. *How to Control the Military.* Garden City,
N.Y.: Doubleday, 1969.

Gamson, William A., and Modigliani, Andre. *Untangling the Cold War.*
Boston: Little, Brown, 1971.

Gardner, Lloyd C.; Schlesinger, Arthur M., Jr.; and Morgenthau, Hans J.
The Origins of the Cold War. Waltham, Mass.: Ginn, 1970.

Gawthrop, Louis C. *Bureaucratic Behavior in the Executive Branch.*
New York: The Free Press, 1969

Gehlen, Michael. *The Politics of Coexistence.* Bloomington, Ind.: Indiana
University Press, 1967.

Gerth, H. H., and Mills, C. Wright, eds. *From Max Weber: Essays in Sociol-
ogy.* New York: Oxford University Press, 1946.

Gilpin, Robert. *American Scientists and Nuclear Weapons Policy.* Princeton, N.J.: Princeton University Press, 1962.

Halper, Thomas. *Foreign Policy Crisis: Appearance and Reality in Decision-Making.* Columbus, Ohio: Charles E. Merrill Publishing Co.,
1971.

Halperin, Morton. *Bureaucratic Politics and Foreign Policy.* Washington,
D.C.: Brookings Institution, 1974.

———. *Defense Strategies for the Seventies.* Boston: Little, Brown, 1971.

———. *The Role of the Military in the Formulation and Execution of National Security Policy.* Morristown, N.J.: University Programs Modular
Services, 1974.

———, and Kanter, Arnold. *Readings in American Foreign Policy: A Bureaucratic Perspective.* Boston: Little, Brown, 1973.

Hammond, Paul Y. *Cold War and Detente.* New York: Harcourt Brace
Jovanovich, 1975.

———. *Organizing for Defense.* Princeton, N.J.: Princeton University Press,
1969.

Hargrove, Erwin C. *The Power of the Modern Presidency.* Philadelphia, Pa.: Temple University Press, 1974.

Heclo, Hugh. *Studying the Presidency: A Report to the Ford Foundation.* New York: Ford Foundation Press, 1977.

Henkin, Louis, ed. *Arms Control: Issues for the Public.* Englewood Cliffs, N.J.: Prentice-Hall, 1961.

Hermann, Charles. *International Crisis: Insights from Behavioral Research.* New York: The Free Press, 1972.

Herring, Edward Pendleton. *Presidential Leadership: The Political Relations of Congress and the Chief Executive.* New York: Farrar and Rinehard, 1940.

Hilsman, Roger. *The Politics of Policy-Making in Defense and Foreign Affairs.* New York: Harper and Row, 1971.

——. *To Move A Nation.* Garden City, N.J.: Doubleday, 1967.

Hoffmann, Stanley. *Gulliver's Troubles or the Setting of American Foreign Policy.* New York: McGraw-Hill, 1968.

——. *The State of War: Essays in the Theory and Practice of International Politics.* New York: Praeger, 1965.

Holsti, K. J. *The Analysis of International Relations.* 3d. ed. Englewood Cliffs, N.J.: Prentice-Hall, 1977.

Hughes, Barry B. *The Domestic Context of Foreign Policy.* San Francisco, Calif.: W. H. Freeman and Co., 1978.

Hughes, Emmet John. *The Living Presidency: The Resources and Dilemmas of the American Presidential Office.* New York: Coward, McCann and Geoghegan, 1973.

——. *The Ordeal of Power.* New York: Atheneum, 1963; Dial, 1964.

Huntington, Samuel P. *The Common Defense.* New York and London: Columbia University Press, 1961.

Irish, Marian D., and Frank, Elke. *American Foreign Policy: Context, Conduct, Content.* New York: Harcourt Brace Jovanovich, 1975.

Jackson, Henry M., ed. *The National Security Council.* New York: Praeger, 1965.

Jacobson, Harold Karan, and Stein, Eric. *Diplomats, Scientists and Politicians: The United States and the Nuclear Test Ban Negotiations.* Ann Arbor, Mich.: University of Michigan Press, 1966.

Janis, Irving. *Victims of Groupthink.* Boston: Houghton Mifflin, 1972.

Jervis, Robert. *The Logic of Images in International Relations.* Princeton, N.J.: Princeton University Press, 1970.

Johnson, Richard Tanner. *Managing the White House: An Intimate Study of the Presidency.* New York: Harper and Row, 1974.

Jones, Joseph Marion. *The Fifteen Weeks.* New York: Viking, 1955.

Kahan, Jerome. *Security in the Nuclear Age.* Washington, D.C.: Brookings Institution, 1975.

Kaufmann, William W. *The McNamara Strategy.* New York: Harper and Row, 1964.

Kelman, Herbert C. *International Behavior.* New York: Holt, Rinehart and Winston, 1965.

Kennan, George. *Memoirs 1925-1950*. Boston: Little, Brown, 1967;
Bantam, 1969.

Key, V. O. *Public Opinion and American Democracy*. New York:
Alfred A. Knopf, 1961.

Kinnard, Douglas. *President Eisenhower and Strategy Management:
A Study in Defense Politics*. Lexington, Ky.: University Press of
Kentucky, 1971.

Kissinger, Henry A. *American Foreign Policy: Three Essays*. New York:
W. W. Norton, 1969.

——. *Nuclear Weapons and Foreign Policy*. New York: Harpers, 1957.

Kistiakowsky, George B. *A Scientist at the White House*. Cambridge,
Mass.: Harvard University Press, 1976.

Koenig, Louis. *The Chief Executive*. New York: Harcourt, Brace and
World, 1968.

Kolko, Gabriel. *The Roots of American Foreign Policy*. Boston: Beacon,
1969.

LeFeber, Walter. *America, Russia and the Cold War*. 3d ed. New York:
John Wiley and Sons, 1976.

Laski, Harold Joseph. *The American Presidency: An Interpretation*.
New York and London: Harper and Brothers, 1940.

Lasswell, Harold D. *The Decision Process: Seven Categories of Functional
Analysis*. College Park, Md.: University of Maryland Press, 1956.

Lepper, Mary Milling. *Foreign Policy Formulation: A Case Study of the
Nuclear Test Ban Treaty of 1963*. Columbus, Ohio: Charles E. Merrill
Publishing Co., 1971.

Levine, Robert A. *The Arms Debate*. Cambridge, Mass.: Harvard University Press, 1963.

Levy, Reynold. *Nearing the Crossroads: Contending Approaches to
Contemporary American Foreign Policy*. New York: The Free Press,
1975.

Lindblom, Charles. *The Intelligence of Democracy*. New York: The Free
Press, 1965.

Litterer, Joseph A. *Organizations: Structure and Behavior*. New York:
John Wiley and Sons, 1963.

Lovell, John P., and Kronenberg, Philip S. *New Civil-Military Relations*.
New Brunswick, N.J.: Transaction Books, 1974.

Lowi, Theodore. *The End of Liberalism*. New York: W. W. Norton, 1969.

Macmillan, Harold. *At the End of the Day, 1961-1963*. New York: Harper
and Row, 1973.

March, James G., and Simon, Herbert A. *Organizations*. New York: John
Wiley and Sons, 1958.

Markel, Lester, ed. *Public Opinion and Foreign Policy*. New York: Council
on Foreign Relations, 1949.

May, Ernest R. *"Lessons" of the Past*. London: Oxford University Press,
1973.

Mennis, Bernard. *American Foreign Policy Officials: Who They Are and
What They Believe Regarding International Politics*. Columbus, Ohio:
Ohio State University Press, 1971.

Millis, Walter. *Arms and Men.* New York: G. P. Putnam's Sons, 1956.

Miroff, Bruce. *Pragmatic Illusions: The Presidential Politics of John F. Kennedy.* New York: David McKay Co., 1976.

Mises, Ludwig von. *Bureaucracy.* New Rochelle, N.Y.: Arlington House, 1969.

Morganthau, Hans J. *Politics Among Nations.* 5th ed. rev. New York: Alfred A. Knopf, 1978.

——. *The Purpose of American Politics.* New York: Alfred A. Knopf, 1962.

Moulton, Harland B. *From Superiority to Parity: The United States and the Strategic Arms Race, 1961-1971.* Westport, Conn.: Greenwood Press, 1973.

Mueller, John. *War, Presidents, and Public Opinion.* New York: John Wiley and Sons, 1973.

Neustadt, Richard E. *Alliance Politics.* New York and London: Columbia University Press, 1970.

——. *Presidential Power.* 2d ed. New York: John Wiley and Sons, 1976.

Nuechterlein, Donald E. *United States National Interest in a Changing World.* Lexington, Ky.: The University Press of Kentucky, 1973.

Nunnerley, David. *President Kennedy and Britain.* New York: St. Martin's Press, 1972.

Ostrom, Vincent. *The Intellectual Crisis in American Public Administration.* University, Ala.: Alabama University Press, 1974.

Paolucci, Henry. *War, Peace and the Presidency.* New York: McGraw-Hill, 1968.

Paper, Lewis J., ed. *The Promise and the Performance: The Leadership of John F. Kennedy.* New York: Crown, 1975.

Plischke, Elmer. *Summit Diplomacy: Personal Diplomacy of the President of the United States.* College Park, Md.: University of Maryland Press, 1958.

Presthus, Robert. *The Organizational Society.* New York: Vintage, 1962.

Quester, George. *Nuclear Diplomacy.* New York: Dunellen, 1970.

Rainey, Gene E. *Patterns of American Foreign Policy.* Boston: Allyn and Bacon, 1975.

Reedy, George E. *The Twilight of the Presidency.* New York: World Publishing Co., 1970.

Ripley, Randall B., and Franklin, Grace H. *Congress, the Bureaucracy and Public Policy.* Homewood, Ill.: Dorsey Press, 1976.

——. *Policy-Making in the Federal Executive Branch.* New York: The Free Press, 1975.

Robinson, James A. *Congress and Foreign Policy-Making.* Homewood, Ill.: Dorsey Press, 1967.

Roherty, James M. *Decisions of Robert S. McNamara: A Study of the Role of the Secretary of Defense.* Coral Gables, Fla.: University of Miami Press, 1970.

Rosenau, James N. *Domestic Sources of Foreign Policy.* New York: The Free Press, 1967.

——. *Linkage Politics.* New York: The Free Press, 1969.

——. *National Leadership and Foreign Policy: A Case Study in the Mobilization of Public Support.* Princeton, N.J.: Princeton University Press, 1963.

——. *The Scientific Study of Foreign Policy.* New York: The Free Press, 1971.

Rossiter, Clinton L. *The American Presidency.* New York: Harcourt, Brace, 1960.

Sapin, Burton. *Contemporary American Foreign and Military Policy.* Glenview, Ill.: Scott, Foresman, 1970.

——. *The Making of United States Foreign Policy.* New York: Praeger, 1966.

Schell, Jonathan. *The Time of Illusion.* New York: Alfred A. Knopf, 1976.

Schelling, Thomas. *The Strategy of Conflict.* Cambridge, Mass.: Harvard University Press, 1960.

——, and Halperin, Morton H. *Strategy and Arms Control.* New York: The Twentieth Century Fund, 1961.

Schilling, Warren R.; Hammond, Paul Y.; and Snyder, Glenn H. *Strategy, Politics and Defense Budgets.* New York and London: Columbia University Press, 1962.

Schlesinger, Arthur M., Jr. *The Imperial Presidency.* Boston: Houghton Mifflin, 1973; Popular Library, 1974.

——. *A Thousand Days.* Boston: Houghton Mifflin, 1965; Fawcett, 1967.

Schurmann, Franz. *The Logic of World Power.* New York: Random House, 1974.

Schwab, Peter, and Shneidman, J. Lee. *John F. Kennedy.* New York: Twayne Publishers, 1974.

Shulman, Marshall D. *Beyond the Cold War.* New Haven, Conn.: Yale University Press, 1966.

Sickels, Robert J. *Presidential Transactions.* Englewood Cliffs, N.J.: Prentice-Hall, 1974.

Simon, Herbert. *Administrative Behavior.* New York: Macmillan, 1957.

Snyder, Richard; Bruck, H. W.; and Sapin, Burton. *Foreign Policy Decision-Making.* Glencoe, Ill.: The Free Press, 1962.

Sorensen, Theodore C. *Decision-Making in the White House.* New York and London: Columbia University Press, 1963.

——. *Kennedy.* New York: Harper and Row, 1965.

——. *The Kennedy Legacy.* New York: Macmillan, 1969.

Spanier, John W. *American Foreign Policy Since World War II.* New York: Praeger, 1968.

——, and Uslaner, Eric. *How American Foreign Policy Is Made.* 2d ed. New York: Praeger, 1978.

Steinbruner, John. *The Cybernetic Theory of Decisions.* Princeton, N.J.: Princeton University Press, 1974.

Stone, Jeremy J. *Strategic Persuasion: Arms Limitations Through Dialogue.* New York: Columbia University Press, 1967.

Strum, Phillipa. *Presidential Power and American Democracy.* Pacific Palisades, Calif.: Goodyear Publishing Co., 1972.

Stupak, Ronald J. *American Foreign Policy: Assumptions, Processes, and Projections.* New York: Harper and Row, 1976.

Taylor, General Maxwell D. *The Uncertain Trumpet.* New York: Harper and Brothers, 1960.

Teller, Edward, and Latter, Albert. *Our Nuclear Future: Dangers and Opportunities.* New York: Criterion Books, 1958.

Truman, Harry S. *Memoirs: Years of Decision* (vol. 1) and *Memoirs: Years of Hope* (vol. 2). Garden City, N.Y.: Doubleday, 1955 and 1956.

Tugwell, Rexford G., and Cronin, Thomas E. *The Presidency Reappraised.* New York: Praeger, 1977.

Ulam, Adam B. *Expansion and Coexistence: The History of Soviet Foreign Policy, 1917-1967.* New York: Praeger, 1968.

——. *The Rivals.* New York: Viking, 1971.

Walton, Richard J. *Cold War and Revolution.* New York: Viking Press, 1972.

——. *Henry Wallace, Harry Truman, and the Cold War.* New York: Viking Press, 1976.

Warren, Sidney. *The President as World Leader.* Philadelphia and New York: J. B. Lippincott Co., 1964.

Warwick, Donald P. *A Theory of Public Bureaucracy.* Cambridge, Mass.: Harvard University Press, 1975.

Wilcox, Francis O. *Congress, the Executive and Foreign Policy.* New York: Harper and Row, 1976.

Wildavsky, Aaron. *The Revolt Against the Masses and Other Essays on Politics and Public Policy.* New York and London: Basic Books, 1971.

——. *The Presidency.* Boston: Little, Brown, 1969.

Wolfers, Arnold. *Discord and Collaboration.* Baltimore, Md.: Johns Hopkins University Press, 1962.

Yarmolinsky, Adam. *The Military Establishment.* New York: Harper and Row, 1971.

Yergin, Daniel. *Shattered Peace: The Origins of the Cold War and the National Security State.* Boston: Houghton Mifflin, 1977.

ARTICLES

Ahmad, Eqbal. "Revolutionary War and Counter-Insurgency." *Journal of International Affairs* 25 (1971): 1-47.

Allison, Graham T., and Halperin, Morton H. "Bureaucratic Politics: A Paradigm and Some Policy Implications." In *Theory and Policy in International Relations,* edited by Raymond Tanter and Richard H. Ullman, pp. 40-79. Princeton, N.J.: Princeton University Press, 1972.

——. "Conceptual Models and the Cuban Missile Crisis." *The American Political Science Review* 63 (September 1969): 689-718.

——, and Morris, Frederic A. "Armaments and Arms Control: Exploring the Determinants of Military Weapons." *Daedalus* 104 (Summer 1975): 99-129.

Bauer, Raymond A. "Problems of Perception and the Relations Between the United States and the Soviet Union." *The Journal of Conflict Resolution* 5 (September 1961): 223-29.

Benjamin, Roger W., and Edinger, Lewis J. "Conditions for Military Control over Foreign Policy Decisions in Major States: A Historical Perspective." *The Journal of Conflict Resolution* 15 (March 1971): 5-32.

Brecher, Michael; Steinberg, Blema; and Stein, Janice. "A Framework for Research on Foreign Policy Behavior." *The Journal of Conflict Resolution* 13 (1969): 75-93.

Brewer, Thomas L. "Issue and Context Variations in Foreign Policy." *The Journal of Conflict Resolution* 17 (March 1973): 89-114.

Bundy, McGeorge. "The Presidency and the Peace." *Foreign Affairs* 42 (April 1964): 353-65.

Carroll, Holbert. "Congress and National Security Policy." *The Role of Congress in the Development and Support of National Security Policy*, edited by U.S. Army War College, pp. 4-14. Carlisle, Pa.: U.S. Army War College, 1969.

Caspary, William L. "The 'Mood Theory': A Study of Public Opinion and Foreign Policy." *The American Political Science Review* 64 (June 1970): 536-47.

Chayes, Abram. "An Inquiry into the Workings of Arms Control Agreements." In *American Defense Policy*, 3d ed., edited by Richard G. Head and Ervin J. Rokke, pp. 321-43. Baltimore, Md.: The Johns Hopkins University Press, 1973.

Davis, Saville. "Recent Policy Making in the United States Government." *Daedalus* 89 (Fall 1960): 951-66.

De Sola Pool, Ithiel. "Public Opinion and the Control of Armaments." *Daedalus* 89 (Fall 1960): 984-99.

Destler, I. M. "Comment: Multiple Advocacy: Some 'Limits and Costs'." *The American Political Science Review* 66 (September 1972): 786-90.

Eckhardt, William, and White, Ralph K. "A Test of the Mirror Image Hypothesis: Kennedy and Khrushchev." *The Journal of Conflict Resolution* 11 (1967): 325-32.

Erskine, Hazel Gaudet. "The Polls: Kennedy as President." *Public Opinion Quarterly* 28 (Summer 1964): 334-42.

Etzioni, Amitai. "The Kennedy Experiment." *The Western Political Quarterly* 20 (1967): 361-80.

George, Alexander. "Bureaucratic Strategy and Presidential Choices." In *Problems in American Foreign Policy*. 2nd ed., edited by Martin B. Hickman, pp. 48-66. Beverly Hills, Calif.: Glencoe Press, 1975.

——. "The Case for Multiple Advocacy in Making Foreign Policy." *The American Political Science Review* 66 (September 1972): 751-85.

——. "The Operational Code: A Neglected Approach to the Study of Political Leaders and Decision-Making." *International Studies Quarterly* 13 (June 1969): 190-222.

Gray, Colin S. "Across the Nuclear Divide—Strategic Studies, Past and Present." *International Security* 2 (Summer 1977): 25.

Hammond, Paul Y. "The National Security Council as a Device for Inter-departmental Coordination: An Interpretation and Appraisal." *The American Political Science Review* 54 (December 1960): 899-910.

Hanrieder, Wolfram F. "Compatibility and Consensus: A Proposal for the Conceptual Linkage of External and Internal Dimensions of Foreign Policy." *The American Political Science Review* 61 (December 1967): 971-82.

Holsti, Ole R. "The Belief System and National Image: A Case Study." *The Journal of Conflict Resolution* 6 (1961): 244-52.

Kalb, Marvin. "What Is Power Doing to the Pentagon." In *Civil-Military Relations and Military Professionalism*, edited by U.S. Army War College, pp. 34-38. Carlisle, Pa.: U.S. Army War College, 1969.

Kelman, Herbert C. "The Role of the Individual in International Relations: Some Conceptual and Methodological Considerations." *Journal of International Affairs* 24 (1970): 1-17.

Kesselman, Mark. "Presidential Leadership in Congress on Foreign Policy." *Midwest Journal of Political Science* 5 (1961): 284-89.

Krasner, Stephen D. "Are Bureaucracies Important? (or Allison Wonderland)." *Foreign Policy* 7 (Summer 1972): 159-79.

Kraus, Sidney; Mehling, Reuben; and El-Assal, Elaine. "Mass Media and the Fallout Controversy." *Public Opinion Quarterly* 27 (Summer 1963): 191-205.

Lindblom, Charles. "The Science of 'Muddling Through'." In *Policy-Making in American Government*, edited by Edward U. Schneier, pp. 24-37. New York and London: Basic Books, 1969.

May, Ernest R. "The Nature of Foreign Policy: The Calculated versus the Axiomatic." *Daedalus* 91 (Fall 1962): 653-67.

Miller, Warren E., and Stokes, Donald. "Constituency Influence in Congress." In *Elections and Political Order*, edited by Angus Campbell, Phillip E. Converse, Warren E. Miller, and Donald Stokes, pp. 351-72. New York: John Wiley and Sons, 1966.

Osgood, Charles E. "An Analysis of the Cold War Mentality." *The Journal of Social Issues* 17 (1961): 12-19.

Peabody, Robert L., and Rourke, Francis E. "Public Bureaucracies." In *Handbook of Organizations*, edited by James G. March, pp. 802-37. Chicago: Rand McNally, 1965.

Pilisuk, Marc, and Hayden, Thomas. "Is There a Military-Industrial Complex Which Prevents Peace? Consensus and Countervailing Power in Pluralistic Systems." In *The Bias of Pluralism*, edited by William E. Connolly, pp. 123-53. New York: Atherton, 1969.

Rosenberg, Milton J. "Attitude Change and Foreign Policy in the Cold War Era." In *Domestic Sources of Foreign Policy*, edited by James N. Rosenau, pp. 111-59. New York: Free Press, 1967.

Roskin, Michael. "From Pearl Harbor to Vietnam: Shifting Generational

Paradigms and Foreign Policy." *Political Science Quarterly* 89 (Fall 1974): 563-88.

Rusk, Dean. "The President." In *U.S. Government Organization and Executive Direction for the Formulation of National Security Policy*, edited by U.S. Army War College, pp. 1-13. Carlisle, Pa.: U.S. Army War College, 1969.

Scott, Andrew M. "The Department of State: Formal Organizations and Informal Culture." *International Studies Quarterly* 13 (March 1969): 1-18.

Verba, Sidney. "Assumptions of Rationality and Non-Rationality in Models of the International System." In *The International System: Theoretical Essays*, edited by Klaus Knorr and Sidney Verba, pp. 93-117. Princeton, N.J.: Princeton University Press, 1961.

Wiesner, Jerome B. "Comprehensive Arms Limitation Systems." *Daedalus* 89 (Fall 1960): 915-50.

Yarmolinsky, Adam. "Bureaucratic Structures and Political Outcomes." *Journal of International Affairs* 23 (1969): 225-35.

York, Herbert. "The Great Test-Ban Debate." In *Readings from Scientific American: Progress in Arms Control?* edited by Bruce M. Russett and Bruce G. Blair, pp. 17-25. San Francisco, Calif.: W. H. Freeman and Co., 1979.

Zimmerman, William. "Issue Area and Foreign Policy Process: A Research Note in Search of a General Theory." *The American Political Science Review* 67 (December 1973): 1204-12.

Zinnes, Dina A. "Hostility in International Decision-Making." *The Journal of Conflict Resolution* 6 (1962): 236-43.

PERIODICALS

Newsweek
The New York Times
Time

INDEX

ABOUT THE AUTHOR

BERNARD J. FIRESTONE is Assistant Professor of Political Science at Hofstra University. He received his Ph.D. from the City University of New York where he studied under Arthur M. Schlesinger, Jr.